Artists' Rescue Tactics

Aberdeenshire Library and Information Service
www.aberdeenshire.gov.uk/libraries
Renewals Hotline 01224 661511

2 8 MAR 2007

1 9 NOV 2010

2 6 MAR 2012

2 1 MAY 2013
- 9 NOV 2013

- 6 DEC 2013

- 4 APR 2016

Artists' rescue tactics

Artists'
Rescue Tactics

How to solve all your painting problems

Collins

First published in 2005 by
Collins, an imprint of
HarperCollinsPublishers
77–85 Fulham Palace Road
Hammersmith
London W6 8JB

The Collins website address is
www.collins.co.uk

Collins is a registered trademark of
HarperCollins Publishers Ltd

10 09 08 07 06 05

6   5   4   3   2   1

© *The Artist* magazine, 2005

The Artist asserts the moral right to be identified as the author of this work.

A catalogue record for this book is available from the British Library.

Designer: Caroline Hill
Editor: Nina Sharman
Indexer: Sue Bosanko

The text and illustrations in this book were previously published in *The Artist* magazine.

ISBN 0 00 718414 X

Colour reproduction by Colourscan, Singapore
Printed and bound by Imago, China

PAGE 1
Plums
TOM ROBB
Watercolour
29.5 × 37.5 cm (11 × 14 in)

PAGE 2
Impression along the Grand Canal, Venice
PAUL BROWN
Oil on canvas
76 × 101.6 cm (30 × 40 in)

▷ *Café du Jardin* (detail)
PETER GRAHAM
Oil on canvas
96.5 × 96.5 cm (38 × 38 in)

PAGE 6
Nottinghamshire Skies
CAROL HODGSON
Pastel
35.5 × 35.5 cm (14 × 14 in)

Contents

Introduction

SALLY BULGIN

Publishing Editor, *The Artist*

Like a good magazine, a practical art book should be both inspirational and informative – you should be able to dip into it at any point and it should catch your attention – which is how I hope our third book, published in collaboration with HarperCollins, will be received.

The idea behind this collection of problem-solving features, originally published in the UK's monthly *The Artist* magazine under the series title 'Rescue Tactics', was suggested to me by Olwen Tarrant, then president of the Royal Institute of Oil Painters. We discussed how practising artists frequently have doubts during the progress of their work, how paintings rarely follow a logical, pre-determined course from start to finish, and how useful it would be for other artists, amateur and professional, to learn more about changes of mind, 'failures', and practical 'rescue' tactics that so often take place during the development of finished works.

Here then you will discover how 20 well-known artists approach a whole range of topics using a variety of different media, and how in each case they adapt their ideas and make practical amendments to their work during its progress. Based on these artistic practices and tactics, they offer help, advice and possible solutions to many frequently asked questions. The book covers a broad spectrum of problems, from the simple adjustment by David Curtis of the composition of a London scene to overcome a too-dominant Nelson's column, to more complex issues such as how Darren Rees overcame a 'lollipop' look in his painting of an owl in the forests of New Hampshire.

A wide variety of subject matter is represented, ranging from people and flowers to landscapes, interiors and still life, and the inclusion of 20 such distinguished artists assures you of a rich source of ideas, styles and inspiration that will be of benefit to painters of all levels of experience.

Sally Bulgin

Dead centre

DAVID CURTIS

To overcome the problem of a feature that was too dominant, the artist adjusted the format, the composition and the weight of tone and colour.

I love the idea of a problem-free painting. It hasn't happened yet! Whenever we embark on a new image there always seems some little niggling doubt as to whether all the various recognized parameters can be adhered to – for example: the best possible compositional value of the given subject; the correct tonal weight or key the image is to be set in; and maybe whether or not we have chosen the optimum light conditions to gain maximum effect from the piece. These considerations, among many others, flash past the mind.

△ FIRST ON-SITE SKETCH
This initial colour sketch helped me to be aware of the elements in the composition.

Composition and light

My commitments in the art world take me to London on numerous occasions and I often feel that so much subject matter lies within the great city, as we dash past on the way to various meetings and exhibitions. Some of the loveliest compositions abound around Trafalgar Square and Piccadilly, especially when enhanced by the clear bright light of sunny days.

The subject matter here takes Nelson's column as the main strong vertical element and using the rather *contre jour* light to its best effect I tried to capitalize on the sweeping diffused shadow emanating from the column to form a sort of lead-in across the pool area in the foreground. I was taken by the light with its magical quality filtering through the fountain further left of the image, but felt that a conflict of interest would develop between it and the column so that the basic composition would not be enhanced by introducing this further element. Often you have to be selective in these decisions and work on the basis of 'less may well be more' in the final analysis.

I tried an initial 'thumbnail' sketch in a portrait format, but the column appeared rather too dominant, so I settled finally for an almost square picture which, for some reason, I really enjoy these days. It seems that when we are searching for that little cameo image the eye tends to see it condensed – a bit like the old 120-photo image.

The first illustration (left), although hastily done, shows a small preparatory colour sketch done *en plein air*, just to get the feel of all the elements in place. I made notes at the same time. In the studio I would juggle the elements around to ensure a satisfactory arrangement.

△ **STAGE ONE**
In this drawn image the
column has shifted just slightly
off-centre to the left to improve
the composition.

Stage one

I noted quickly that the column in the first sketch
was probably rather too centrally placed and so
decided to shift its position just slightly off-centre
to the left. This, I think, does help the composition.

It was a tricky drawing exercise, particularly in
the foreground structure of the fountain's side
walls. If you try this yourself, you will see what
I mean. Curving elliptical shapes are a real
problem and have to be observed and measured
carefully to convince the eye that a true sense of
perspective exists across the foreground feature
of the water surface.

This is a very 'busy' subject with lots of figurative
interest and little in the way of restful areas to
allow the eye to settle across the image. One way
of forcing this simplicity was to make less of the
distant buildings around Admiralty Arch. This
decision was eased by the existence of the scaffold

△ **STAGE TWO**
It is important to set the tone and colour value of the painting, at this early stage, by applying an overall wash.

cladding, the likes of which envelop so many buildings in the city these days. I thought, originally, that this might be an unattractive feature, but by treating the whole area on the left merely as a diffused silhouette, it became sufficiently convincing.

Stage two

A little carefully placed masking fluid was applied to some strongly lit passages, before the application of an overall wash designed to set the tone and colour value of the painting. The wash was adjusted warm to cool, dark to light, in one intensely concentrated experience. The final outcome of a painting is decided quite often, I feel, by the success of this first-stage wash. If you get the essence of all colour pretty well placed, you're halfway there. This technique affords a really sound foundation for the subsequent stages and if it feels

◁ **STAGE THREE A**
All the masking fluid is
removed to reveal the white
highlight areas.

right, then the ensuing confidence in the process
can yield a successful final result if you keep the
mind focused all the way.

Stage three

This stage addresses the removal of all previously
applied masking fluid after the work has dried
thoroughly (above) and the placing of a few strong
dark elements in order to set the extremes of tonal
value (right). So, therefore, we have preserved
highlights (white paper), diffused mid tones and
some of the darkest darks stated.

Stage four

Further detail was addressed at this stage, and
I was careful to be economic with the degree of
'fussiness' employed. Don't paint every window in
full form and detail, but rather paint a suggestion
or amalgam of the whole, observing little reflected

△ **STAGE THREE B**
This detail shows a few of the
strong, dark elements that
have been added.

◁ **STAGE FOUR**
Further detail is added, without being too fussy, and a few figurative elements are introduced loosely in the middle distance.

▷ **FINISHED PAINTING**
Autumn Light, Trafalgar Square
Watercolour
27.8 × 25.3 cm (11 × 10 in)
This lovely composition was enhanced by the clear bright sunshine. Nelson's column is the main strong vertical element and I capitalized on the sweeping diffused shadow emanating from the column to form a sort of lead-in across the pool area in the foreground.

areas where this would be advantageous, as you can see on the group of buildings on the far right.

You will note that the sun is almost directly behind the column and so a diffused warmth is evident around the edges of the column structure. Softening the edges with a little cadmium orange or lemon yellow creates a sense of a glow that almost wraps round the solid form. This must be done with great subtlety and is especially effective here against the sky area.

Also at this stage I have started to introduce a few figurative elements, mainly to see how they relate to the whole. Certainly, at middle distance they are merely suggested loosely – more definition being reserved for the little groupings in the foreground.

Finished painting

With the essentials now in place, I felt I must now extract more of the character and atmosphere of

the subject. Thoughtful positioning of the groups of figures really assists the sense of scale and pattern. Rather than painting a series of individuals, I like to paint small groups, using a single varied wash to fuse the overall shapes together as a mass. You so often see this in reality and the effect can be achieved by this technique, adjusting warm to cool, with the weight of colour forced at some points and more fluid in others, but retaining some light punctuations, so completing the overall general shape. The group of six or so people best illustrates this technique.

A real weight of tone and colour is reserved for the foreground pool structure. It draws the eye forward and so lends a sense of space to the further distant elements. An overall bluish wash encompasses the foreground, which is essentially a cast shadow from the column. The top-lit surfaces of the wall, which in Stage three was left as virgin paper, now receives a

gentle wash of warm colour to complete the foreground light effect. One or two warmer punctuations such as the red London bus, and the flags at ease, I hope suggest a still autumn day.

The essential challenge was to extract the sense of activity and movement, and suggest, rather than overstate, the filtered light effect as it was presented on the day. It is so easy to make a statement in paint which is safe and laboured, while losing the immediacy and visual joy of an image one is really enthusiastic about exploring.

To crop or not to crop

JACKIE SIMMONDS

This composition of two dancers caused problems but the technique of cropping presented the artist with a number of potential solutions.

Although my preference is usually to work from life, there are times when this is not possible and I have to work from sketches and photographs to produce my images. These images will begin with an idea sketched out as a thumbnail. Thumbnail sketches work well for me on the whole, and I use them whether I am working from life or from

△ **THUMBNAIL SKETCH**
Pencil sketch of proposed composition
10 × 10 cm (4 × 4 in)
This very rough, small sketch composed of the main elements of the scene helped me to develop the basic design in the form of a tonal plan and to discover the pattern of light and dark areas.

reference material. I ponder my sketches and my photographs (or the scene before me) and eventually set to work, developing the basic design in the form of a tonal plan – a very rough, small sketch composed of the main elements of the scene, searching out the pattern of light and dark areas within the rectangle.

I also look out for the opportunity to create, or exaggerate, echoing shapes, and I try to explore the underlying geometry of the image. Thumbnail sketches are usually black and white, and produced in either charcoal or a soft pencil. I don't often do colour studies because I like to keep some elements of the work flexible; too much preparation, for me, can lead to a rather stiff result. Instead, I try to sort out the colours in the painting from the mental image I have of the finished piece. If this turns out to be a bit of a struggle, I don't mind this too much (well, I do at the time, but afterwards I tell myself it was worth it) because out of the struggle, the painting sometimes develops extra depth and richness through the overlaying of pastel marks and colours.

My ballet images, a new theme for me, are mostly being developed in this way because of the difficulties of working on the spot. I do some rough sketching, and take loads of photographs. I do not directly copy photographs because I would find that a rather sterile activity; in fact, I believe that the creativity in all paintings, whether they are done from life or from reference, depends on the artist's ability to move beyond mere mimicry.

Dancer series

For this series of dancer paintings I returned to life drawing classes to improve my drawing. I sketched

and photographed backstage and in rehearsal
studios, and also worked with a dancer model at
home. I wanted to put two figures together and
asked my dancer to pose in two different ways, so
that I could construct the painting from the two
poses. The thumbnail sketch had promise and
I decided to tackle this image as a large pastel.

I loved the potential of two figures together.
I liked the echoing shapes and angles created by
the legs and arms. I liked the way the dress of the
standing dancer provided a light-coloured shape
against the dark background, while the tutu of the
seated dancer was dark-coloured against the lighter
floor – a nice element of counterchange.

However, the girl on the floor gave me huge
problems. No matter how often I drew and redrew
her, there was always something about the pose that
bothered me. Maybe it was her arms – they seemed
awfully long. And perhaps too wide, too. Maybe it
was the stiffness of the pose; she couldn't hold it for
very long so I photographed her, and perhaps the
camera distorted the pose because I was shooting

△ STAGE TWO
Tracing paper is placed over the
pastel, and felt-tip pen used to
draw around the shapes at the
bottom of the image.

down towards the floor. Photos do tell lies! Maybe it was the lack of emotional connection between the seated and the standing figure. Whatever it was, I was not satisfied with the result.

Using cropping as a solution

In the end, I decided to try a rescue technique: cropping. Many artists resort to this from time to time; it is a good way to discover, within an existing image, different compositions or options. I suggest you try it: take two L-shaped mount pieces and play around with them on an existing image, perhaps one that displeases you. See how many new compositions you can find.

It wasn't so easy to do with my dancer pair, because the seated girl's legs overlapped the chairs in the picture. So before taking the drastic step of removing her in the hope that it might be a good solution, I took a piece of Schminke pastel tracing paper, and drew over the appropriate section of the image, replacing the dancer's legs with chair legs and some of the floor.

I used a felt-tip pen on the tracing paper for this exercise, and then worked over the top with my

▷ STAGE THREE
The new section is roughly
painted with pastels and then
cut out.

pastels. Then I cut out the appropriate portion of the tracing paper, and dropped it down again on to the painting, and replaced the L-shaped edges to see what the new image would look like.

I liked what I had achieved, although I realized immediately that I would be rather sad to lose my seated dancer. But unless I could correct the drawing to my satisfaction I was prepared to crop and repaint. With pastels, this is not too difficult to do. I would simply take a stiff brush to the picture, brush off the dancer, fix the area, and add more pastel.

◁ **STAGE FOUR**
The tracing paper section is placed over the picture and mount pieces are placed over the top. Now we can see quite well how the cropped picture could look.

◁ **ALTERNATIVE TO CROPPING**
Still in 'rescue' mode, trying out a change to the seated model on tracing paper, changing the head so that she looks up at the seated dancer. The result gives, to my eye, better emotional content, so it might be worth a try before I take the drastic step of cropping.

△ **SECOND PASTEL**
Fixing her Hair
Pastel on paper
33.5 × 45.6 cm (14 × 18 in)
My doubts about the figures
on the right encouraged me
to see how the painting would
look if they were cropped
away. I scribbled lightly over
the areas which would show
any crop.

Creating new compositions

Cropping to produce a completely new image, one
that not only works within the rectangle but also
pleases my inner taskmaster, may well be the better
option rather than modifying the painting in some
other way. This is the approach that I used with the
second image, *Fixing her Hair* (above), where I was
uncertain about the figures on the right. I decided
to see how this painting would look if the two
figures were cropped away. As with the first
painting in the dancer series, I will take a fair
amount of time to consider this idea.

Cropping is, perhaps, a rather drastic way to
'correct' an unhappy picture, but it can often

△ **PROPOSED CROP**
This is how *Fixing her Hair* could look without the two dancers on the right. I think this is, perhaps, the best version. However, before cropping, I will take some time to consider this idea.

produce wonderful results. Finding new images by cropping feels very creative, too – it is a satisfying thing to do. From a larger picture, particularly one that you feel has failed, or doesn't meet your own high standards and please your inner taskmaster (we all have one, don't we?) you may find a number of other, more concentrated, intimate compositions, with a good strong balance of shapes and tones.

3 Transformation of a still life

ANUK NAUMANN

A failed watercolour painting can form the basis of a new piece of work with careful thought and the use of collage and acrylic colour.

Of all the possible subjects for painting, the still life most satisfies a magpie mentality. I am attracted to the jewel-like colours of fruits in season, and I hoard 'treasures' in my studio which will one day appear in a new composition; the blue and white jug, the lace tablecloth, the various coloured glass vases all adding up to a kaleidoscope of possible ideas. I also hate to waste anything, and there is seldom, if ever, a painting which is thrown away; instead it is stored, to be re-used in part or as a whole to contribute to a new piece of work.

The painting *Blue Hydrangeas* (right) began life as a watercolour demonstration to an art group. While explaining my techniques of washes and wet in wet I concentrated on the blowsy blue flower heads, and was reasonably happy with the result, although I was never totally satisfied with the composition, so into the plan chest it went, to await the germ of another idea.

Mixing media and using collage

Over the years of painting I have experimented with various techniques. Always painting in water-soluble colour, I have used a variety of media progressively in my work, with collage, acrylic and pastel combined in multiple layers to achieve the texture and effect I want. And so, with these ideas and techniques in mind, I decided to 'rescue' *Blue Hydrangeas* and bring it more into line with the style of painting I produce today.

Collage is an ideal medium for such a rescue, because layers of papers can be applied to obliterate the image beneath and create a new surface on which to work. As I liked the actual heads of the hydrangea flowers, I decided that these should remain, and the rest of the painting

△ **ORIGINAL PAINTING**
Blue Hydrangeas
Watercolour
36 × 36 cm (17 × 14 ¼ in)
I was never content with the composition of this painting, so into storage it went, to await transformation.

◁ **STAGE ONE**
Returning to the painting,
I began to introduce collage
and gradually the blue and
white vase of cornflowers
began to disappear.

would be created around them. Stage one (above) shows how I began to collage over the other elements of the picture which I thought were too fussy, covering them with random papers. Gradually the blue and white vase of cornflowers began to disappear and I started to introduce some new elements. A stylized flower pattern on a piece of wrapping paper took my fancy and I decided to include it to the left of the picture. A new component such as this can take my thinking about the final painting into another direction,

which is all part of the excitement of using papers, selected at random and torn into shape.

Changing the format

As I worked, selecting some areas to retain and others to obliterate, I began to reassess the whole composition. I wanted to make more of the feature that I had saved, namely the blue hydrangeas, and decided that to do this I needed to crop the painting. I tend to opt for a square format in my current work, both for still life and landscape

The painting is now a square format and the vase of hydrangeas has become dominant. Using collage, I darkened the background to bring the leaves and flower heads to the fore. In so doing, I altered the shape of the vase.

paintings; I like the ambiguity of not having a dominant proportion.

When I made the crop a sudden, dramatic change came over the picture (above): the vase of hydrangeas became dominant, as I wanted, and virtually filled the whole picture plane.

With some more collaging I began to darken the background to bring the leaves and flower heads to the fore. In applying this last bit of collage, I simplified and changed the shape of the vase, straightening out its curves so that it was more in keeping with my final composition.

Once I was satisfied that I had put as much texture into the painting by means of collage as I wanted, I applied gesso – in some areas clear and in others coloured – to the surface of the work (right). I had now laid down a suitable surface for further painting, which was done with acrylic colour. The use of gesso helped me to simplify shapes within the picture even more, and to create planes of colour into which I could work with

different layers of paint. In this way, I reduced the shape of the vase to a simple cylinder and removed all the other distracting components of the picture.

The elements of the composition were beginning to become abstracted, with the hint of a white tablecloth appearing, and already the painting had moved a long way from its rather cluttered beginnings.

With the gesso applied and left to dry, it was time to 'rediscover' the picture with paint. I knew that I wanted to finish up with a painting that had a feeling of warmth and richness, and so I began to apply layers of yellow ochre and orange to the left-hand side, with a corresponding darker area of blue and purple to the right. With each application of paint I lifted off some of the colour with screwed-up newspaper, a method known as 'tonking', to reveal the colour underneath. This gave a rich feeling of depth, which together with the texture applied previously, broke up the surface in an interesting way.

Creating a new composition

As I simplified the composition I began to emphasize the use of squares and rectangles, breaking up the background into these geometrical shapes. In the initial painting there was a suggestion of a window behind the still life, so I reintroduced this with a loose representation of houses in the top-centre background square, which is light ochre in colour, the whole giving the impression of evening sunlight coming through an open window.

And what of the elements that I have taken away from the original painting? The cornflowers have gone and I decided not to bring these back to the final painting, but to balance the flowers. I have included a bowl of fruit as before, this time a bowl of pears rather than clementines, which I felt would sit more happily with the ochres of the background. I have also 'rescued' the small blue and gold coffee cup and placed it to the left of the painting.

At this stage I wanted to reintroduce orange that served as a complementary colour to the blue hydrangeas, originally in the form of the clementines. Taking a bold step, I transformed the white cylindrical vase into an orange jug, and balanced its strength with some carefully placed squares of the same colour towards the top of the picture. With the strength of the colours in the background, the heads of the hydrangeas, which I had carefully preserved, were beginning to look rather washed out, so I strengthened them and added touches of corresponding pastel colour in the form of lines to the left of the painting.

When faced with the problem of a painting that has not worked in the way I would like, I invariably turn to the use of mixed media. As can be seen in this example, areas can quickly be covered over and altered, while leaving key elements behind. The use of collage and acrylic can give a strength of colour and texture to a painting that was not there before, and the judicious use of cropping can dramatically alter the emphasis. In these ways, a failed painting can be given a new lease of life.

◁ **STAGE THREE**
Gesso was used to prepare the surface for painting. It also helped to clarify the shapes and to create planes of colour. It was time to transform the picture with acrylic colour.

△ **FINISHED PAINTING**
Blue Hydrangeas
Acrylic and collage
36 × 36 cm (14 ¼ × 14 ¼ in)
As well as the change in
format, the composition
has been simplified, partly
with the use of geometrical
shapes, and partly by replacing
certain elements and
changing colours.

The hawk owl

DARREN REES

Areas of disharmony can be problematic, particularly in wildlife paintings, but by searching for missing elements the artist achieved unity and atmosphere.

Paintings will always pose problems for the artist. It's a matter of how you deal with the problems, or indeed recognize the problems, that dictates the success of a piece of work. To take a three-dimensional world and represent this in two dimensions is no straightforward task. The learning process for any subject is founded upon problem solving, and art is no different. With paintings the problems may be fundamental, such as a misunderstanding of perspective or tone, or just plain bad drawing; or perhaps be more subtle and concerned with issues of design, colour pitch or unity. Whatever the problems, failure to recognize them as they arise will result in failure to learn. Sometimes we must be a little hard on ourselves if we want to develop our skills.

The evolution and execution of this particular piece of work illustrates the problems that I face.

Wildlife encounters

All my paintings of wildlife are a result of encounters in the field, both at home and abroad, and in this case I was leading a winter bird-watching group to New England, looking at the rich variety of birds found at this time of year on America's northeast coast. Among them are huge rafts of sea duck and large birds of prey, most usually associated with Arctic territories. These include birds that, for the bird-watcher, hold near-mythical status, such as the powerful gyrfalcon, the incomparable large white snowy owl and one that had always eluded me, the charismatic hawk owl. Imagine my excitement, then, when we were told that a hawk owl had been seen in the mountains of New Hampshire, some three hours' drive from our hotel. The hunt was on!

As we drove north into the White Mountains National Forest, the temperature dropped considerably. When we left the warmth of the mini-van and started our search the thermometer reading was minus seven degrees Celsius. A friendly local, complete with cowboy hat, pointed out where the owl was and soon I was watching the bird of my dreams. Time to start sketching.

Working compositions

The starting point for the painting began with an examination of the sketches taken from the field. I had some poses (below and on page 26) that I thought I could develop and carry forward into a studio piece.

Sorting out a working composition is easier to do on a small-scale watercolour study; all my large studio pieces start their lives in this form. If wholesale composition changes are needed, or

PENCIL SKETCHES
These sketches of the hawk owl were done in the field.

△ **FURTHER PENCIL SKETCHES**
More poses of the hawk owl that became the starting point of the painting.

indeed if a composition needs to be abandoned, it is best done at this stage.

The initial compositions in watercolour (right) came to me when watching the hawk owl. They have a high horizon off the top of the image and so concentrate the viewer's attention on the bird and its immediate surroundings. Further, these are true to the image I could see as I was watching the owl through a high-magnification telescope. This crops the panorama and compresses the perspective to focus on the subject and a small area around it. I wanted to tell the complete story, though, and looked for an alternative composition.

The forests in the White Mountains change at different altitudes. The hostile environment at the tops of the mountains results in a dwarf vegetation with no trees. This terrain above the tree line is snow covered for most of the winter, giving rise to the mountains' name. A narrow belt of stunted, low-growing krummholz forest exists just below the tree line and this is regularly dusted with snow throughout the winter months, giving the zone a frosted look. The forest covering the lower slopes, where I was watching the owl, was a mixture of dark peaked spruces, taller conifers and standing dead trees. I wanted a composition that would relate the whole experience of being within these bitter boreal forests; a composition that would portray this wilderness of distinct terrains.

◁ **COMPOSITION WITH LARGER LANDSCAPE**
The forests of the White Mountains change at different altitudes – from dwarf vegetation higher up to dark peaked spruces and tall conifers on the lower slopes. I wanted a composition that would portray this wilderness of distinct terrains.

How much sky?

I thought that another composition featuring the owl perched high on a tree with the larger landscape behind might be preferable (see page 28). But how much sky should I show? Too much would leave a smaller area in which to describe the rich texture of the forests. Too little would result in the owl being framed by the trees and not the sky. Surely, to give the feel of a single bird perched in a bare tree scanning a lonely landscape, it would be desirable to use a lot of space around the owl.

I would usually agree with the old adage that a horizon line cutting a picture in half should be avoided. However, as the mountain skyline here is far from horizontal I chose a roughly midway position for the division of sky and forest. As the owl is the primary focal point, the landscape can take second place. Indeed, a precise placement of the horizon at one third up or one third down can result in an over-constructed painting lacking naturalism.

Choice of painting medium

Having settled on a composition I started on the painting, choosing to use acrylic. I often prefer this medium for larger works, particularly those with a predominantly landscape element. I work very quickly and tend to build up layers to achieve interesting textures. This is easy with acrylics as the successive layers are dry, whereas with oil the wet layers can get confused and muddy. I also scumble thin layers of translucent paint over thick layers of opaque to modify colours and create texture. This is to be avoided with oils as 'lean over fat' can result in cracking.

Acrylic can be used on a variety of supports and I use both canvas and board. For larger pieces, where boards would be liable to warp or are just too heavy, I use traditional canvas. For *Hawk Owl, Winter* I chose a panel of MDF. This was primed with several coats of gesso, which I applied with a decorator's brush. This was done with alternate horizontal and vertical strokes to create a crisscross texture. The ground colour was a crimson red, chosen as a complement to the cool blues and greys that would dominate the painting.

I started building up the image by blocking in the main elements of sky, mountain, forest, and the bird with its perch. The sky was put in with bold strokes of both palette knife and brush, with mixes of ultramarine, burnt umber, Naples yellow and titanium white. I brought some of these strokes through to the forest area to bind the image together. In both sections I let the ground colour of red break through in a random fashion, again helping to unite the separate elements of the painting. The mountain was blocked in with thick strokes of neat white, taking these strokes below

ALTERNATIVE COMPOSITIONS
In these three studies the owl is perched high on a tree with a larger landscape behind. The question I asked myself was how much sky should there be? Too much (above) leaves a smaller area to describe the forests. Too little (left) results in the owl being framed by the trees and not the sky. I decided to use a lot of space around the owl (below) to give the feel of a bird perched in a bare tree scanning the landscape.

the tree line to the area that would represent the frosted zone. The peak could be modified with clear glazes of greys, while the high forest could be drawn in with dry brush work from mixes of ultramarine blue and alizarin crimson.

Putting in the bird was done with constant cross-references to the live sketch. It is important to keep in mind that, although this is essentially a pale bird with barred markings, the overall tone is dark. It is, after all, just another solid form against the sky.

The bulk of foreground forest was built up more slowly. The mid-distance trees could be suggested with many small repeated brush strokes, but the nearer trees would have to be drawn with more care. The dark conical crowns of spruces were painted with a mix from olive green and ultramarine. These shapes could be altered with pale green passages cutting in to the tree profile with the result that the final spruces were a blend of positive and negative painting. I had to make sure that the forest appeared as one continuous swathe of trees, so the pale dead trunks would diminish in size and brightness as they swept into the mid-distance. Similarly, I was constantly bringing colours from one area to the other to harmonize the scene.

Missing elements

The painting (right) was nearing completion and indeed remained at this stage for a long time in my studio. Something was missing, though, and it took some time for me to decide exactly what it was. Quite often I will have several paintings on the go at any one time. By leaving a piece alone for a while (sometimes several months), one can return to the image with fresh eyes and readily see areas of disharmony within the painting.

It is important to me that my works stand up for themselves as paintings in their own right, and not just as illustrations of the wildlife I have had the opportunity to see. One feature of hawk owls as they perch in trees at invariably low temperatures is that their plumage is fluffed up to preserve body warmth, so much so that the observer never sees the bird's feet. This can look strange to the untrained eye. My bird, although faithfully observed, looked as though it was stuck on the perch like a lollipop,

rather than naturally sitting there. I decided to extend one of the top twigs and take it through the feathering just beyond the outline of the bird. The eye now reads the bird as balancing.

Also missing was a crucial, unifying element to the painting. As I was watching the bird and sketching, snow flurries would come and go, some brief and some more sustained. If I were to remain true to the encounter, then I needed the confidence and conviction to add a snow squall. After some

△ ACRYLIC PAINTING
Although much of the painting is complete, something is missing. I left the painting at this stage for some time before returning to it in the hope of identifying the areas of disharmony.

trepidation, and a lot of practice flicks, the painting was laid flat and then splattered with opaque white from a large decorator's brush. The result was immediate. A few hand-painted flakes here and there over the body, and the owl was now amidst the snow flurry. All that was left was to modify the light falling on the bird so that it was consistent with new situation. Here was the unity and atmosphere I was seeking. The painting was complete. Problem solved.

Back to the beginning

PAUL DERBYSHIRE

Washing off unwanted colour and returning to the original concept allowed the artist to capture the Hong Kong skyline in watercolour.

Some people are supremely confident and like to dive straight into a watercolour painting, conceiving it on the page, but I prefer to work out the composition with a number of small pencil sketches first. This doesn't mean I stick rigidly to the composition, as the painting may take many twists and turns during the course of completion. Serendipity often plays a role, but unfortunately not all artistic accidents are happy ones. If you make a mess it doesn't mean that you have been wasting your time and your picture must be scrapped, as there will be many avenues you can take and maybe end up with something far more exciting and creative.

After painting in the same steady style for many years you can find your work is becoming dull and lifeless and you are getting bored with it. I suspect that many of us are fearful of departing from the security of familiar ground, but experimentation and mistakes are the life blood of progression.

I find it helps to try different materials from time to time, new approaches and, if you can bear it, a change of subject matter (says he, who cannot drag himself away from images of Hong Kong, though I do alternate between landscape, seascape and cityscape). Even so-called artist block is really a sort of wake-up call.

Whenever possible it helps to use good quality materials as, apart from durability, it is amazing the difference this makes, especially in ease of use (but note that I haven't used the most expensive for the painting New IFC, Hong Kong, shown here). My method of working means that I actually need fairly heavy paper of good quality, though watercolour purists would eschew my techniques.

Reference videos and photographs

For many years I have been taking my annual holiday in Hong Kong, staying with members of my family. From the moment of the first hair-raising descent between the high-rise buildings towards the reclaimed land of the runway (with sea at the end and side) of the now demolished Kai Tak Airport, I have been entranced with the place – the frenetic activity of city life, the ebb and flow of shipping against the backdrop of modern architecture, the outlying islands, hills and awe-inspiring countryside dotted with traditional Chinese buildings.

I usually endeavour to do a considerable amount of drawing to ascertain the shape and form of the subject matter, supported by videos and photographs, so that I have a great amount of reference to work from. I stress that these only act

△ **AIDE-MÉMOIRE**
This photograph was taken more or less facing north towards Kowloon, new Territories, mainland China, with the IFC (left) unfinished when I was there in 2002.

For this picture I used Arches Aquarelle 140lb (300 gsm) paper with Reeves French ultramarine watercolour, mostly diluted, to map in the picture as a whole. I worked all over the painting at the same time, leaving only the areas that I wanted to remain white. The paint was applied broadly with a three-quarter-inch Series 50 Arton brush.

as an aide-mémoire and source of inspiration, as I rely on memory to a great extent and prefer to concentrate on the essence of the subject matter and not on the exact details. I manipulate the forms to suit my particular composition or mood and frequently tilt the horizon and vertical forms to a more interesting angle.

Last year I was not able to make the trip and in my absence another skyscraper has been completed, changing the harbour frontage which I knew so well and have painted many times.

Luckily, my family have come to the rescue and provided enough photographs for me to appreciate the impact of this new interloper and, with the aid of this new reference material, I was able to embark upon the painting of the International Finance Centre (IFC). I wanted to paint this building, which is over 400 metres (1,312 feet) high and not as attractive as some, to show how it now dominates the Hong Kong skyline; the previous tallest was the Central Plaza at 378 metres (1,240 feet).

Getting started

I always stretch my paper first, regardless of its weight, as I know it will probably be receiving some rather robust treatment, and while it is drying I work out the composition on a scrap of paper.

Firstly, I mapped in the picture as a whole. I prefer to work all over the painting at once, flitting here and there, trying to keep an all over progression, rather than one bit at a time. In the first instance I didn't touch the areas that I wanted to remain white. I also added touches of Winsor & Newton Cotman alizarin crimson at strategic points (Stage one).

Creating atmosphere

Dusk falls very quickly in Hong Kong and I wanted to create that particular time of day when everything is beginning to sparkle, is less sharp and the city begins to emit its evening glow. My aim was to show the impact of the IFC against the Kowloon waterfront, with the New Territories landscape and China beyond.

I applied varying amounts of Cotman cadmium pale yellow hue, to suggest the lit areas and used a mixture of Winsor & Newton Prussian blue, a touch of Reeves French ultramarine and a very small amount of alizarin crimson to create a night effect.

Having done this I realized that I hadn't captured the light-polluted atmosphere that I was aiming for and that the contrast was too great, so rather than proceed in this direction I decided to return to my original concept.

◁ STAGE TWO
I wanted to show the IFC against the Kowloon waterfront with mainland China in the background. I soon realized that I hadn't captured the light-polluted atmosphere and decided to return to my original concept.

◁ STAGE THREE
After protecting the white and yellow areas with poster paint (and once this had dried) I took the picture to the shower and just allowed the water to rinse off the unwanted colour. This shows just how effective the treatment was in reverting the picture back to (almost) its original state.

At this stage I wanted to keep many areas white and the yellow as clean as possible, so I protected them with inexpensive white poster paint, including the outside edge of the paper. I prefer to keep this surrounding edge clean because any marks close to the picture can be distracting. I allowed this to dry thoroughly. I could have protected those areas with gum arabic or masking fluid, but both of these are expensive and there was rather a lot of area to cover.

I took the picture to the shower, being careful not to scuff or tear the paper, and just allowed the water to rinse off the unwanted colour. The poster colour was washed away at the same time, but not

After intensifying the picture
with more Prussian blue and
French ultramarine, I used
touches of Cotman cadmium
yellow pale hue and alizarin
crimson to establish the
feeling of the bright lights and
the neon signs emerging,

before it had protected the specified areas. It was then lightly blotted and dried quickly with a hair drier and I also checked the gum strip to see if any of the tape had become unstuck.

I returned to intensifying the picture with more Prussian blue and French ultramarine, combined with the use of finer brushes: a three-quarter-inch 50 Series Arton, and a Winsor & Newton Series 33, No. 3 Sable. I also used touches of Cotman cadmium yellow pale hue and alizarin crimson to establish the feeling of the office lights and the neon signs beginning to emerge (Stage four).

Detail and balance

By now I was mainly concerned with building up the detail while making sure that the balance of the whole was maintained and that parts of the picture did not leap forward too much. However, it is still important to try to create recession by accentuating the detail in the foreground and tailing this off as it moves through the middle ground to the distance. I added varying amounts of Winsor & Newton titanium white watercolour (Stage five).

Using artistic licence

During the development of this picture I had been aware that it could almost be of any built-up

harbour, as the new IFC building, although huge, was not saying, 'This is Hong Kong', so I had been toying with the idea of using artistic licence by introducing the well-known and exquisite Bank of China (which in reality would be out of the picture to the east) into order to play off these buildings against each other.

With this in mind I had left a ghostly image in the right foreground and during the final stage I decided to go ahead and include the bank, but because any added white watercolour would sink into the dark colour, I once again used a little gum arabic under the areas where I would add the white filigree. Again, rapid drying was called for to prevent sinking, or the under-painted blue leaching into the white. This done, I then intensified the surrounding blue, and the blue reflected in the glass, to bring the bank and the whole foreground forward, therefore gathering importance in the picture.

◁ **STAGE FIVE**
By this stage I was concerned with building up the detail while making sure that the whole balance was maintained and that parts of the picture did not leap forward too much.

▽ **FINISHED PAINTING**
New IFC, Hong Kong
Watercolour
41 × 55 cm (16 × 21 ¾ in)
The overall feeling of the picture was enriched by using a very thin wash of ultra blue Dr P H Martin's Concentrated (liquid) Watercolour.

6 Invention and improvisation

JOHN LIDZEY

By bold scrubbing, masking out and repainting, the artist not only improved watercolours of floral subjects but also added a spontaneous quality.

Painters have always been attracted to flowers as a subject for their work. Many have created images of floral reality with such incredible detail that the viewer is almost tempted to touch an insect on a leaf to see if it is real. I can only wonder at such technique, but have never really wanted even to try to emulate it. I am not interested in absolute realism, as such: it is the relationship between paint and the subject which interests me most.

△ **ARTISTIC LICENCE**
I used masking fluid roughly to block in most of the flowers, and then painted loose washes over to define the general shape of the flowers and vegetation. Extra washes were laid one over the other in an improvisational fashion, adding details of leaves and grasses to suit the look of the overall composition.

A chief interest is the way watercolour can behave in the process of description so, when it comes to painting flowers, I am usually preoccupied with its capacity to create effects with runs and stains that evoke the lush florescence of plants.

I prefer painting wild flowers rather than the cultivated variety. Daisies, poppies, cow parsley, buttercups, campion, snowdrops and aconites have for me a quality which might be seen as a metaphor for the transient nature of life. As Wordsworth put it: 'The meanest flower that blows can give thoughts that do often lie too deep for tears.'

Mostly I prefer to set flowers among contrasting objects or unusual surroundings. A favourite way of working is to set loosely painted wild flowers against an ordered, carefully delineated background. My studio equipment, for example, makes a wonderful complementary setting.

Flowers can also have added interest when arranged in an unconventional container. In *A Watering Can of Flowers* wild flowers, grasses and other vegetation were stuffed into a watering can. The display was one of lush florescence but it lacked tidy compositional form and a certain amount of artistic licence and invention was necessary to make the painting work.

Because I am interested in the effects of light, I often paint flowers on an interior window sill. If the window is in sunlight this can make a particularly good subject.

Pre-planning

Before I begin work on a watercolour I have only a general idea about how the painting might look. I frequently make preliminary sketches to help me determine an angle of view and a possible lighting

◁ **FINISHED PAINTING**
A Watering Can of Flowers
Watercolour
28 × 24 cm (11 × 9 ½ in)
I wiped away paint, repainted,
and softened the detail. After
removing the masking fluid
I washed colour over the flowers
and added extra detail. I used
white gouache for floral effect.

effect, but all too often the finished painting departs from my original intentions.

Many painters plan their work thoroughly and stick to their plan. The matter is different with flower subjects. I often find that a painting takes longer than a day and goes on to a second or even a third, when blossoms inevitably droop, leaves wilt or something else disturbs the arrangement. On such occasions I am obliged to improvise or even invent replacement flowers or foliage. It can also become necessary to make adjustments to the composition to make the painting work effectively.

Improvisation can impart a fresh, spontaneous quality to flower paintings, but mistakes can occur

which may need alteration. But sometimes through a happy piece of serendipity the end result is better than anything which might have been planned.

Scrubbing out

This is a method I use to eradicate parts of a watercolour I do not like. It is possible to wash out complete backgrounds with cotton wool, a sponge or even a scrubbing brush. It is easier to wipe out paint while it is wet, especially when the colours are of the non-staining variety, but even watercolour that is dry can be partially or completely removed.

Very occasionally I have laid down a substantial wash as a background for a painting only to

▽ FINISHED PAINTING
Garden Corner
Watercolour
28 × 21.5 cm (11 × 8 ½ in)
I wiped out many areas of colour: foreground, yellow left-hand leaves, ground to the right-hand side of the boot and the boiler shaded area. I repainted the left-hand leaves in green. The foreground was indicated with more concentrated stippled paint. After the paint had dried I used white gouache with cadmium yellow to suggest some pale yellow flowers. I added some green foliage to the right of the boiler and tidied up the busy lizzie leaves. The painting now had a tighter construction with a more satisfactory colour balance, the busy lizzie flowers were now a focal point of the painting.

△ TIME TO RETHINK

A concrete boot, planted with primulas, had been placed next to an old steel boiler and what looked like a stone turtle. The foreground was a mixture of rough grass and weeds with a yellow-leafed plant. I wasn't sure how to treat these areas so just freely brushed on watercolour to fill the spaces.
I laid down dilute carmine for the left hand busy-lizzie flowers and a pale green for some of the leaves and painted masking fluid over the top. The boot itself and the shadow areas were loosely brushed in. So far so bad!

discover that a different colour would be more suitable. Rather than begin again I have scrubbed the wash out. The result has been a grainy, faint texture which has provided a useful base for the new colour wash.

Washes applied over scrubbed-out areas can have a quality which is unobtainable on fresh paper. The act of rubbing out can often make the edges of subsequent washes bleed in an interesting way. Do not attempt to scrub out paint on papers less than 140lb (300gsm) or you may have a hole in your work. Also, even on heavier papers don't be too heavy handed or you may damage the paper.

Altering the colours and tonal values in the course of a painting can often be a way to make a painting work. It becomes possible to manipulate the elements to achieve a satisfactory compostion in the finished watercolour (see *Garden Corner*).

I have often scribbled Conté or pastel over areas of paint I did not like. Obtrusive or fussily painted items can in this way be held back quite successfully. To make a floral subject appear more colourful I have sometimes hatched black Conté crayon over background features (see *A Jug of*

△ **ORIGINAL PAINTING**
Studio Flowers
Watercolour
17 × 13 ½ in (43 × 34 cm)
The curtain added nothing to the picture and was not well painted. Also, because of the large areas of low tones (top left, bottom right) it had a rather gloomy appearance. Originally I had felt that a billowing curtain would create a sense of mystery but on completing the painting I saw that I had just made a simple subject much too complicated.

◁ **FINISHED PAINTING**
Studio Flowers
Watercolour
10 × 11 in (25.5 × 28 cm)
This painting now works much better. The composition is greatly improved; the subject of the painting is not fighting the background nearly so much.

▷ **MIXED MEDIA**
A Jug of Flowers
Watercolour and crayon
28 × 20 cm (11 × 8 in)
This watercolour seemed to
work quite well except that
I didn't care for the foreground.
The shelf and white table edge
seemed to slice off the
bottom right-hand edge of the
picture. I could have masked
off the lower edge close to the
left-hand bottle, but I felt that
this would have made the
glass jug too low in the picture
area. I decided to break up the
diagonals to a small degree by
scribbling black Conté crayon
over them. I also smudged an
arbitrary patch of cadmium
red at the base of the painting
to draw attention away from
the diagonals still more.

Flowers). Doing this not only kills detail, but it can impart a vigorous sketch quality to the watercolour. Paintings which I have given up for lost have sometimes been made to work, albeit in a way I didn't imagine at the outset of painting.

Masking out

In many cases after spending time and effort on a painting it turns out as a disappointment. However, remasking can turn a possible failure into some

kind of success. I have often identified a small part of a large 'failed' watercolour, cut it down and remasked the part which I considered to be successful – snatching a victory from the jaws of defeat (see *Studio Flowers*, page 39). I have also remasked a disappointing painting, scaled it down gradually until, when it was reduced to the size of a postage stamp, I have given up and consigned the work to the bottom drawer of the plan chest, marked 'Odds, Ends and Failed Experiments'.

A portrait's progress

ALASTAIR ADAMS

In order to attain the elusive final image, the artist reworked previously painted statements, incorporating new ideas and approaches, in this painting of a family group.

Sometimes people are surprised when I turn up to paint their portrait without my paints. I believe in getting to know the person first. From this foundation, as a relationship and knowledge grows, a true portrait will evolve. The final painting is the end result of a natural, progressive response to the sitter and their surroundings. A physical likeness can be achieved quite quickly from a sitting in a studio, but I believe each person has their own unique composition waiting to be discovered.

Composition development

Any creative process involves interaction, development, judgement and assessment. Painting is no different. As time passes, and situations and images present themselves, it is natural for the artist to respond, develop and change ideas in an attempt to attain the perfect, elusive, final image. Many avenues have to be explored and, according to his or her judgement, the artist must be prepared to re-work previously painted statements in the hope that the painting will evolve into something different, yet more appropriate.

This is quite normal. As artists we must always be open to looking at subjects from various perspectives, incorporating new ideas and approaches, and be ready to re-think and alter accordingly. Sometimes a big re-work, involving many hours, may be a hard but necessary decision to make, especially when on the surface there seems to be nothing wrong with a painting.

Initial statements are not necessarily incorrect; a painting may just need more time and the benefit of hindsight. Often my commissioned portraits start as loosely drawn pencil sketches that I hope capture my ideas and offer a flavour of the final painting. Sometimes artists can't explain ideas to a client, and a rough sketch at this stage can speak a thousand words. Agreeing on a rough composition and feel is important: it is necessary to get the fundamentals right from square one.

Sitting one – preliminaries

The original rough drawing for this family group of three was completed after the first meeting. Often it is not until my return journey that first impressions start to sink in and relevant ideas for

△ SITTING ONE
In this rough drawing of the family group everyone sat next to each other on the sofa with an empty seat at one end. The sitting room was chosen for the location as it seemed to be the most natural setting in which Mary, her daughter Rachel and son Richard could be themselves.

As I set about sketching and got to know the sitters, with their strong personalities, it became apparent that the previous composition, posed in a row, no longer seemed appropriate. When Richard sat forward, he created an engaging foreground lead into the picture and I was quick to use this and the table top to help suggest space.

△ SITTING THREE
Working in acrylic, I began by painting in large areas of simple observed colour. I find that colour subtlety and richness is best attained by building up successive layers of paint.

compositions present themselves. I wanted to depict a close-knit, young, lively family.

Something, however, did not seem right; someone was missing. As the commission was a birthday surprise for the father, despite being an integral part of this family's character, he could not take part. To address this I placed everyone close together on the sofa with an empty seat at one end, and my subjects looked out, perhaps inviting him to join in. For a location I chose the family

◁ **SITTING FOUR**
At this point I undertook a
re-working of Rachel's pose
as I felt she looked out of
character. She is now more
relaxed and I have drawn
attention to her bare feet.
Trying to make Mary unique in
the composition, I introduced
an individual colour.

sitting room. It wasn't the most formal room in the house but seemed the most natural setting for my kind of painting and a natural habitat in which mother Mary, daughter Rachel and son Richard could be themselves.

Sitting two – sketching

With these ideas in mind the composition was agreed and at the next sitting I set about sketching the group and surroundings. Usually I start drawing on one piece of paper and add to the edges with more, depending on where the drawing leads me. When I'm back in the studio this can be cropped to suggest several formats.

As I drew, and the sitters moved around, it became apparent to me that all had quite strong personalities and led individual lives. The previous composition, posed in a row and looking straight ahead like a football team, no longer seemed to fit. From a picture-making point of view everyone was on the same plane with their legs chopped off and there was little depth. By contrast a greater level of interaction and character now seemed to be emerging. At one point Richard sat forward on the sofa, creating an engaging foreground lead into the

picture and breaking out from the flat planes of the previous composition. I was quick to use this and the table top to help suggest space from such a steep viewpoint.

Sitting three – using acrylic colour

Before my third visit, with the aid of my drawing and some photographs, I drew up the new composition back in the studio. On location I start by painting in large areas of simple observed colour. Depending on the commissioner's preference, I usually work in acrylic as it seems to suit my working method best. I find that colour subtlety and richness is best attained by building up successive layers of paint. Experience told me that in a composition of this nature there would be many.

Sitting four – reworking

While continuing to work further on Richard as a strong central figure, I began to feel the need to offset him against Mary and Rachel. I undertook a major re-working of Rachel's pose as I felt she looked out of character and too submissive, making her more laid back and making more of her bare feet. I also tried to introduce an individual colour

△ **SITTING FIVE**
Here I adjusted the pose of
all three sitters. Rachel's new
pose suggests interaction with
the others. Richard's legs
seem to work better with
Mary's feet. Once Mary began
to sew I felt that she fitted in
better. In addition, I made
changes to the table in the
foreground, the sofa, the
window and I moved the piano.

for Mary that would make her unique in the
composition but still work in the overall design.
My main focus for the next sitting was to be Rachel
and Richard, as they were soon both to leave for
the summer.

Sitting five – making changes

Once again I found it necessary to change Rachel's
pose. Previously she looked squashed into a corner
and as if she were fighting with Richard. Now
I wanted to make yet more of her feet and suggest
more interaction.

Richard's pose also changed slightly so that his
legs would work better with Mary's feet. He had
just returned from school, so ended up with black
trousers. Mary began to sew, a favourite pastime of
hers, and seemed to fit better in this new position
in the picture plane. To accommodate these
changes, I decided to reduce the size of the table
in the foreground, widen the sofa, increase the size
of the window and move the piano.

Sitting six – light and shadows

Further alterations were made to Mary, whose
presence was now beginning to take shape. With

a tilt of the head she now draws Rachel's gaze. More light was painted in to try to lift the shadows further. As the main light source in the painting is from the back coming forward, the foreground could get murky and shadows at the front of the sofa and around the feet needed special attention.

Often for the sake of maintaining authenticity compromises have to be made and the opportunity to make use of stray reflected light can be a real bonus. During the course of a day's sitting I found the foreground would be illuminated first thing in the morning and last thing in the afternoon, hence

△ DETAIL OF SITTING SIX

the direction of the shadows. I painted an old knitted toy, of some relevance to one of the sitters, on the back of the sofa. Often a device like this can unlock many stories from the past.

Studio time

Prior to the last sitting I like to spend some time in the studio making sure I've got the thinking straight. At this stage it can be hard for me to take an objective view of the painting. By backing off and letting the portrait stand, any niggling faults have time to come to light. I'm also fortunate enough to have friends who drop in and give me feedback, often from a very objective point of view. This time in the studio can also be used to take care of more repetitive detail such as the keys on the piano, the texture of the carpet, the detailing on Richard's shirt or the pattern on the sofa.

Final sitting

Although I still try to leave myself open to quite fundamental changes even this late in the day, usually the final sitting is spent tying up loose ends and creating the finishing touches. To give the painting a specific date I have included a copy of

△ **FINAL SITTING**
The Findler Family
Acrylic on board
137 × 152.4 cm (54 × 60 in)
During the final sitting I tied
up some loose ends and
created the finishing touches.
The old woollen toy is now
being mended by Mary, which
makes its presence seem
less deliberate.

the Wimbledon week Radio Times. Mary is now
mending the old woollen toy, which gives her
something poignant to work at and makes its
presence seem less deliberate. As the finer details
of Mary's, Rachel's and Richard's faces are worked
on, their true natures are revealed.

The portrait is only finished when, by a process
of elimination, trial and error and the passing of
time, I know I can say no more without needing
to produce another painting. It is the natural
culmination of a process of interaction resulting
in a single statement.

It is rare in my work to see initial marks forming
the body of the painting, instead they become one
of the many layers and textures that chart the
development of a relationship reflected in paint.

Rising to the challenge

JAMES HORTON

Recreating the past is a formidable task, as the artist discovered during the development of this commissioned painting set in the Edwardian period.

The development of any painting is always of the greatest interest, especially to fellow painters. One stands in front of a picture in a gallery and wonders how the artist arrived at that point. What did it look like, say, halfway through? Did the painting get better as it progressed or were there periods when it began to slip away? More importantly, if a picture does begin to slide out of your grip, what can you do to pull it round?

These are questions that every painter grapples with most of the time and of course the answers are just as elusive as they have always been. The reality is that as painters we are perennially involved with and captivated by the process of painting rather more than by the finished article. Of course, we all

have favourite pictures that we admire and like to contemplate, but it is only a question of time before that question pops up: 'How did the artist do that?'

Exactly how any of us do what we do is a vexed issue. How often has a picture gone well, but when you try to repeat the success it just won't happen. This is always frustrating and not least a little strange because you feel you should be able to retrace your own footsteps. One thing is certain: the development of a painting is never straightforward and never runs to plan.

In the painting *The Old Bury Bakery* (see page 51) there is a bit of a story attached. This was a commission from a physiotherapy practice who, having bought a building for redevelopment,

◁ **STAGE ONE**
This was the first attempt at placing the figures within the room. Given the dimensions of the room, and what I needed to show, it was almost like having a stage upon which to place my players.

wanted to commemorate the bakery before it was lost. The idea was to show the bakery in its heyday, which was, roughly speaking, the Edwardian period.

Researching your subject

With pictures taking a route that is not always straightforward, or as you would like it to be, I know very well that if you are to stand any chance of achieving your aim, you must at least begin with some sort of tangible aim. Otherwise, things will certainly never go to plan. In the case of *The Old Bury Bakery*, in addition to the usual compositional problems, I had the task of researching the costumes and being faithful to the architectural proportions of the room and the features of the ovens.

In essence, if a painting like this is to succeed, then everything right down to the smallest detail has to be well rehearsed and thought out. If not, the prospect of moving a figure or part of the architecture once the painting is well established, could be a nightmare. However, having said that, planning and experimenting with scale, placing and lighting has enormous scope in the early stages and provides a great deal of enjoyment.

Like many other painters, I am at my best when working from life, and the great challenge of this picture was to be able to paint as much as possible from actual people and objects, even though it was an entirely imaginary scene. Once I had researched the costumes sufficiently, I set about getting them made up using the right sort of material, roughly stitched together, that would make the appearance satisfactory to paint from.

The next step was to get my son to put on the outfits and try out a few poses. Because the lighting in this picture was of paramount importance, the positioning of the figures created a range of shadows, different each time the figure moved. Armed with some basic information about poses and a knowledge of the architecture of the room and position of the ovens, I could now begin to piece together a composition.

Placing the figures

One of the central features of the painting was the Victorian ovens, which had to be shown, more or less, in their entirety. This put certain restrictions on the way the figures would be assembled around them. Right from the start I envisaged two bakers: one in the act of taking loaves out of the oven and the other looking on, possibly waiting his turn to work. The third figure would be a woman assistant,

▷ **STAGE TWO**
In this second attempt, I tried altering the stance of the main baker to see what effect that had on the positioning relative to the ovens. The two other figures remained relatively the same.

▷ STAGE THREE

In this sketch I introduced some wash and the beginning of floor ties to gain a little more idea of the bulk of the composition.

stacking the loaves. I arrived at the position for the woman fairly quickly, as there seemed to be less choice as to how she would appear. The two bakers changed positions several times until I arrived at the final choice.

Originally I had imagined the left-hand figure supporting himself with his arm resting on the oven, which is how he appears in the early composition drawings. Also the central figure adopts a much more dynamic pose in the first sketches, almost as if he is jousting. It was only after going back to a live model and double-checking the stance of both figures that I realized neither looked right.

Having arrived at a positioning that I felt was workable, I then got to work squaring up and transferring the image to canvas. In fact, I rarely 'square up' these days, preferring to use a pair of proportional dividers. These enable you to set the small end to the drawing and when adjusted correctly the larger end will automatically open up to the right size. This has the advantage of ensuring that the right proportion from small to large is maintained, but leaves plenty of scope for original drawing rather than religiously following a squared-up drawing.

As I prefer to work from life whenever possible, my fully articulated lay figure comes in very useful. For each of the three figures I dressed the dummy very carefully in the appropriate clothes and then placed the figure in the correct relationship to the source of light. I actually own a Victorian gas lamp like the one portrayed and was able to position it the correct distance from the window and place the lay figure accordingly. Being able to work in this way is essential for a painting of this sort, observing all the subtleties of a warm gaslight and the much cooler daylight.

Regarding the figure on the left, I found that the colour of the shadow cast on the wall varied from a green grey to a purple/blue grey depending on how far from the wall he was placed. Observations such as this are vital if the painting is to carry any conviction. The lay figure also provided an added bonus – there was no need for rests, feeding or any sort of financial remuneration.

Still-life collection

As for the shelves on the far right of the picture, I had no idea what would actually be on them until I came to paint the area. Having arrived at this point I selected a collection of Victorian objects

In this sketch the baker on the left achieves his final position. Somehow the raised arm did not look convincing and it seemed more natural that he would balance it on his waist. Having gone back to a live model, the stance of the central baker becomes more appropriate to the function he is performing rather than looking as though he is poking some unseen foe with this long pole.

and set them up as an actual still life, in the correct source of light, in the studio. I then painted straight from life until the area was complete, making the final adjustments at the end of the whole painting to make sure it arrived at the same pitch as the rest of the work.

Opportunities for change

Although it cannot be said that a painting of this sort changes a great deal during its progression on the canvas, there are many opportunities in the design stage for changes of mind. Later on, once work is underway, there are actually a great deal of changes that take place in respect of colour. Once the painting takes shape and you begin to get more involved with colour values, the balancing act of how one colour appears against another becomes increasingly important. For example, the intensity of the red on the floor tiles changed several times, as did the area of shadow surrounding the gas lamp and how that shadow met the daylight coming in from the window. The first statements that you put down with all confidence and faith very often have to be corrected or adjusted once the overall impact of the painting gains momentum.

No painting ever stands still, or just becomes a matter of filling in – or at least it shouldn't – because if that happens all the joy of exploring, adjusting and balancing is lost. Due to the various component parts in this picture that needed balancing, both in colour and tonal pitch, the amount of adjusting and discovering how one passage affected another was considerable. Had the composition and general tableau not been well tried and tested I would never have been so free to enjoy the process of the actual painting.

△ **FINISHED PAINTING**
The Old Bury Bakery
Oil on canvas
96.5 × 122 cm (38 × 48 in)
The first statements you put down frequently have to be adjusted once the overall impact of the painting gains momentum. For instance, the left leg of the central baker comes back even further than before, and supports his weight more effectively in this final version. And in respect of colour values, the intensity of the red of the floor tiles changed several times.

9 Unwelcome elements

BARRY HERNIMAN

Choosing the perfect view can be difficult, but by juggling with reality the artist was able to overcome initial problems of composition in two contrasting subjects.

Usually there are a million paintings just around the corner, but striving to find something out of the ordinary to get down on to paper can obscure the ordinary scene. Painting *en plein air* is more exhilarating than painting indoors; however, choosing the perfect view can become tricky. A photograph takes only a microsecond, so you are able to stand in the middle of a lane or on a wall to get your photograph, but painting is different in that it takes time, and your spot has to be chosen more carefully.

Normally you can find the view you want without too much trouble, but every now and then getting a good composition means juggling with reality. If you come across a wonderful view but there is an unwelcome element that spoils it, then artistic licence says, take it out!

Initial inspiration

On a short day trip to York I was presented with typical problems of composition. Having walked along the city walls I caught an inspiring view of the Minster with its two towers almost face on, the large square tower on the left. There were some lovely brick houses in front of the Minster and because of my elevated position on the city wall I was able to look over the rooftops to the Minster (top left). However, this view was marred by a great slab of chimney right in front of the right-hand tower, so I moved along to an almost perfect spot with all the chimneys in the right place and the towers at a nice angle – but now couldn't see anything because of all the foliage that hung down over the scene (far left).

Moving even further to the left of the cathedral I got quite an open view with a very interesting roofline to the right. The main tower was separated from the two towers rather too much now to make a pleasing composition (left).

Working in the studio

Once back in the studio I set to work to try to salvage some order from the scene. First I drew a very rough outline sketch of the cathedral using

▷ **UNWELCOME CHIMNEY**
This first inspiring view of York Minster was spoilt by a great slab of chimney directly in front of the right-hand tower.

△ **RESTRICTED VIEW**
In this second photograph all the chimneys are in the right place and the towers are at a nice angle – but now the scene is marred by too much foliage.

△ **OPEN VIEW**
Although my third attempt gave me a more open view with a different roofline, I was still not completely satisfied with the composition.

the first photograph as a reference. I then took the roofline from the second photograph with its nice chimney stack to the left, which made a good frame for the cathedral.

Before going into the sketch with a lot of tonal shading I made a few photocopies of the original line drawing that I could then work on without having to keep redrawing the cathedral.

Next I took the roofline from the right of the third photograph and added it to my sketch (below). The buildings in front of the cathedral were multi-storied and quite tall so I elongated

△ ROUGH SKETCH
Using aspects from the first and second photographs, I made a very rough outline drawing of the cathedral. Based on the restricted view photograph, the roofline includes the chimney stack to the left, which helps to frame the cathedral.

▷ STRUCTURE FOR PAINTING
With the roofline from the right of the third photograph and the elongated buildings in front of the cathedral in place, I had the framework. I hatched in the main tones and added a little foliage at the top of the picture.

the scene to get a feeling of height. Once I had the framework in place I used a 4B pencil and hatched in the main tones. I added a little foliage at the top of the picture to pull it together. I now had the structure for a painting that I felt quite happy about.

Man-made obstacles

Kerne Bridge – Wye Valley presented me with a different type of composition problem – a view marred by a man-made obstacle. As you can see from the Polaroid (below), this wonderful view from Coppett Hill is spoilt by an electricity junction box. The problem with many point-and-

shoot cameras is that their wide-angle lenses really compact the scene in order to get a lot in. The result is a clear view of the electricity poles but the river and bridge pale into insignificance. If when you returned home this was the only reference you had, it really wouldn't inspire you to paint the scene. So if you do use a compact camera without a zoom lens, make sure that you have some sort of sketch to back up your photographic reference to avoid being disappointed later.

I took the second photograph (below left) with my standard lens, which is better for seeing something of the bridge and river, but still isn't great. So I moved to the right and with my zoom lens zoomed in on the bridge (below). Now I had what I was looking for.

Before I did any painting I went straight in and did a tonal sketch (right), getting rid of all the

△ **POLAROID REFERENCE**
A wonderful view is spoilt by an electricity junction box; the river and bridge pale into insignificance.

△ **STANDARD LENS**
This second photograph shows more of the bridge and river, but is still not what I was looking for.

△ **ZOOM LENS**
I moved to the right and with my zoom lens zoomed in on the bridge. Now I was pleased with the result.

extraneous bits of leaf and branch that were still in the way. I did this sketch on a square piece of paper, hence the format, but I wanted to do the painting in a portrait format.

Using a piece of 300lb watercolour paper I sketched out the main skeleton of the scene with a 2B pencil. Graphite sticks are great for tonal sketches but when it comes to painting in watercolour I like to keep pencil work down to a minimum.

I applied masking fluid to the main highlight areas – the water in and around the bridge – across the top edge of the bridge and also in the path on the left-hand bank.

Once the pencil work had been completed I sprayed the paper lightly with a spray atomizer. This keeps the paper slightly wet and helps to keep the paint flowing.

Watercolour stages

Now with my basic colours, aureolin, cobalt blue, and rose madder, I started to lay in my first washes, keeping the whole area fluid and mixing paints on the paper. Having dropped some darker accents of cobalt blue and brown madder into the bridge I then started to lay down some fluid washes into the water area (Stage one).

When the initial washes are being laid in they sometimes go into unwanted areas. When this happens you can lift out the colour with a dry tissue in the area you want cleaned (Stage two). When the paint is wet and running you can lift out without any worry about harsh lines.

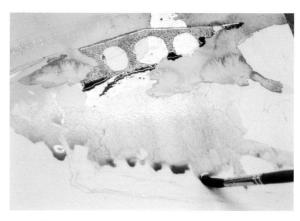

△ **STAGE ONE**
I began by laying down some fluid washes into the water area.

△ **STAGE TWO**
The initial washes ran into unwanted places so I used a dry tissue to lift out the colour, where necessary.

△ **TONAL SKETCH**
I got rid of all the extraneous bits of leaf and branch that were still in the way and sketched out the main skeleton of the scene with a 2B pencil.

△ STAGE THREE
Here you can see an area in
the foreground that has been
lifted out. I liked the area of
highlight in the water so
I decided to leave it in.

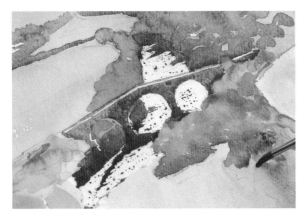

△ STAGE FOUR
Once the initial washes were
dry, I started to lay in a darker
area around the river trees.

After the first overall washes had been applied the paint was allowed to dry completely. You can see an area in the foreground that has been lifted out (Stage three). This was because I put the initial washes on the bankside trees too quickly and they merged with the still damp wash of the river; an unsightly 'cauliflower' formed just above the trees as a result. I lifted out the cauliflower, leaving an area of highlight in the water that I thought worked rather well – so I left it throughout the painting.

With these initial washes bone dry I started to lay in a darker accented area around the river trees with Indian yellow, aureolin, brown madder and cobalt blue (Stage four). I kept a loaded brush and moved the paint around the paper.

With a smaller, No. 8, brush I started to lay in the shadow areas of the bankside trees, before working into the main bankside tree areas with a No. 3 rigger, starting to form a 3D effect using a darker mix to establish the shadows (Stage five).

All the masking fluid was removed in the river/bridge area (Stage six). Notice how stark white it is! Be careful when applying a mask at the beginning as it can severely ruin a really good painting with its 'white worm' appearance later on.

When you are working quickly some areas will dry faster than you would like and harsh lines can appear. This was the case with some of the tree clusters in this painting, so I gently scrubbed the offending area with a damp brush and once the dried paint had started to move I moved the paint around to negate the harsh edges (Stage seven). Do not use a tissue at this stage, or a sponge, as this will lift all the paint from the paper and leave a white area. By using a damp brush the paint is softened and the colour remains.

Then I was able to go back into the tree areas and drop in the shadows, working my way down the painting to the bankside trees in the foreground, putting in darker shadow colours as I went (Stage eight).

Next, I flicked some colour into the foreground to bring it forward, keeping the brush an inch or so from the paper and tapping the brush handle to produce a nice 'spatter', (Stage nine).

Finally I lifted out the masking fluid from the bankside path, dropped in a little Indian yellow to give this area a lift, and cleaned up the loose edges.

△ STAGE FIVE
Next I began to lay in
the shadow areas of the
bankside trees.

△ STAGE EIGHT
Then I went back into the
tree areas and dropped in
the shadows.

△ STAGE SIX
The masking fluid was
removed in the river/bridge
area – it is now stark white.

△ STAGE NINE
To bring it forward, I flicked
some colour into the
foreground .

△ STAGE SEVEN
Some of the tree clusters
dried too fast and harsh lines
appeared, so I gently
scrubbed them off with a
damp brush.

▷ FINISHED PAINTING
(OVERLEAF)
Kerne Bridge – Wye Valley
Watercolour
50.8 × 40.6 cm (20 × 16 in)
I added a little Indian yellow
to lift the bankside area.
The initial problem of
composition has been
overcome and the river and
bridge are now clearly the
focus of attention.

10 Second thoughts

TOM ROBB

The artist deals with two unsatisfactory watercolour compositions, making a fresh start with one, and adding colour washes to the other.

Changes occur naturally – few paintings end up exactly how we imagined before starting. But sometimes the results are simply too weak, too far from the original idea, and they turn out to be unsatisfactory, even on their own terms. We've put in time and effort, but to be honest, it hasn't worked.

When this happens, put the offending paper away for at least a couple of days and then take another look. Try to blank out what you first planned and see the painting as something quite new, with no pre-determined opinion in your mind. If it has that vital core and stands up in its own right, albeit not in every aspect, then it is worth thinking about what might be missing, and how you could work a little magic to make the potential come true.

At worst, if after a couple of days you cannot see any fundamental value, then perhaps even magic is not enough and the whole concept was perhaps a mistake. But normally you should find enough that will give you a good new start.

There are many reasons for a painting to be unsuccessful – a lack of scale, or perspective, or satisfying composition, for example – but I want to concentrate on the use of colour, one of the most powerful tools in any artist's vocabulary. It's the element which can trip up even established artists, and yet it's also the easiest to fix, once you have recognized the problem. Colour can change, be made stronger or be or played down, and a very small shift can have an extraordinarily strong effect.

This can be seen in the history of two different paintings of mine, one of which, *Plums* (right), had wonderful colour but somehow didn't read at all well, and the other, *Street in Minorca* (page 61), with too little colour that looked bland and pointless.

Plums

The fruit from the market was so gorgeous, so lusciously purple, that I sat down that very afternoon to paint. I laid on Winsor violet as a beautifully liquid wash, adding a white plate full of reflected purples to contain them. Waiting for the paper to dry I was really pleased.

But as the first satisfaction wore off, I became more objective; the paint dried and I saw that the

△ **INITIAL WATERCOLOUR**
My first attempt emphasized the deep violet colour of the plums with Winsor violet and ivory black with a tiny touch of the violet on the background. This proved to be at the expense of everything else, and the painting simply didn't work. They were nice rich plums, but they were out of kilter with the rest, and without any focus.

▷ FINISHED PAINTING
Plums
Watercolour
29.5 × 37.5 cm (11 × 14 in)
Here I kept the plum colour softer and added a lot more water to increase the light touch; the yellow open plum started out a little too bright, so I toned it down a bit. The plate was outlined in ultramarine, again using plenty of water, the shadows deeper at the side and in colour rather than black. In fact, all the colours, background as well, were kept light and fruity without any black in the mix. I felt much happier with this, and went on to do more studies – until all the plums were eaten.

painting somehow just didn't work. True, the purples were right, the rounded shapes were right, the lovely feathery edges were right, but the result was simply too dull. Trying to heed my own advice, in spite of a pang of disappointment, I put the pad down for a few hours and worked on another project, managing to avoid the temptation to eat all the plums (I did have one) and destroy the set-up.

The next morning I started again, and saw at once that in spite of the violet, there was no glow or sparkle; something was needed. I added darker shadows, but that only made it worse. The plate seemed to float on the background, too. I felt I could do much better, but by now, with all the fiddling and changing, I wouldn't be able technically to remove enough of the washes to allow me to start again.

The set-up still looked interesting and I wanted to try to get it right. Remembering the colour of the inside of the plum when I bit into it, I cut one open to show the yellow flesh, and it only needed a shadowy raw umber for the stone. Remembering the blue shadows of Cézanne's still lifes, I underlay the white plate with blue, and suddenly I could see that the painting was coming alive. Now everything was heightened, the colour had become more vibrant with the contrasting tones, and the plums

were, if anything, even more tempting. The whole colour palette had shifted into a different key.

Street in Minorca

The second painting is very different. I had made the original sketch on the spot in Minorca, working quickly in the very strong midday sunlight. The glare was so harsh that although what I painted was a fair interpretation of the scene, the result was a jumble of irregular shapes in grey and white. Bland, meaningless: not a success!

Almost as soon as it was finished, it was clear that even as an abstract pattern it was unsatisfactory. The sun had blinded my eyes to all the subtlety and variation that was in the street. Luckily I had also taken a photograph, which gave me a few clues, and I was also able to go back the next day at a different time of day to see if I could rescue the work that I had put in the previous noon.

Early the next morning the sun was more kind, and I could now see colour where before I had seen only glare. The first job was to lift the worst of the shadows. I sponged the areas carefully, although there was no necessity to go back to the white paper; the need was plenty of soft sepias and greys and a few washes of pink and brown. These immediately

turned single blocks of space into rows of individual buildings. Now I could see a flash of yellow ochre high up near the tower. I made the flash into a more substantial roof, and that single yellow stroke transformed the whole street.

The green evergreen shrubs and trees had been almost black; I added a little more green and softened their outlines.

And finally, without the midday heat there were a few people strolling out to do their shopping; adding these as quickly-sketched figures emphasized the scale of the buildings as they gently rose up the hill.

Can it be rescued?

The first lesson in rescuing a painting is that sometimes you do need to start again. This may mean a complete new version, but keep your concept. You should always learn from any failed attempt. From the plums, for example, I found that

△ **LEFT-HAND DETAIL FROM ORIGINAL SKETCH**
This small section shows in detail why the painting simply didn't look like anything: the buildings were too light; the trees too dark. Once I began to add shadows in various tones, that single stretch of white plaster turned, as it was in reality, into a row of quite individual houses. This also made a much better balance with the dark trees.

▷ **RIGHT-HAND DETAIL FROM ORIGINAL SKETCH**
This is another detail where I had the right splash of colour – the yellow roof – but the houses were too vaguely defined, and it all blurred into a pale nothing.

colour need not be brilliant or eye-catching; it had just as delicious an effect when the whole palette was lighter and brighter.

The second painting taught me never to work in direct sunlight, especially in hotter climates; it will affect your perception of colour as well as intensify the shadows. It is also a common mistake to make shadows too dark so that they dominate the rest of the painting. Any interesting details will be blocked out. However, if the basic composition and subject are in place, by adding some very subtle washes, everything in the sketch can be transformed, delineated and made substantial. Watercolour is the perfect medium for this.

Don't give up when something doesn't work. You may have to start a new painting but the second attempt is often better. Or it may be that by looking more carefully and doing more work on your original painting you can rescue a mediocre work and find something truly satisfying at the end.

11 Achieving lift-off

WINSTON OH

From sponging off colour to drastic cropping, the artist reveals his techniques for turning unsatisfactory watercolours into successful compositions.

Making alterations and corrections in watercolour can be challenging, compared with working in opaque media such as oils, pastels or gouache. A watercolour painting laid down in one, or preferably not more than two, washes has the unique quality of clarity and luminosity. When dry, washes have distinct edges, and corrections can be difficult to mask completely. The purist will say that any correction would spoil or devalue a watercolour and it would be best to discard it and start again.

Well, not all watercolour painters are purists, and most of us are still learning the process. Making a correction usually means one has recognized a defect and therefore will have learnt something from the exercise.

Tonal values

The two most frequent changes I make are the reduction and enhancement of tones. I am constantly aware that whatever intensity of colours are used in a painting, the relative tonal values should remain within a certain range to achieve an harmonious composition. For example, a painting of a misty morning should contain a narrow range of tones, whereas a painting of a sunny afternoon against the light will test the extremes of tones, but nevertheless stay within an acceptable range.

With these principles in mind, I may tone down a foreground cloud shadow that is too dark against the rest of the picture, or a cast shadow on the side of a white building that is also dominant. A tree or stand of trees in the middle distance may be excessively dark, unbalancing the composition (see original painting, *Temple of Apollo, Stourhead, Wiltshire*, right).

Some artists resort to immersing the entire painting in a basin of water in order to soften tones. When tones are judged to be too light, or some counterchange is required, I lay another wash of the same colour and perhaps add a glaze of dilute cobalt blue or French ultramarine if the area is in shadow (see *Bracciano, near Rome* page 66).

Where distant objects are not cool enough, such as hills or woods that are brown, green or too grey, I lift some of the colour out, and when the painting is completely dry, I may lay a glaze of blue or grey-blue over them. Foregrounds or other segments that require a stronger tone need only an additional layer of the same colour, perhaps

△ **ORIGINAL PAINTING**
As it was a sunny day, the colours were bright and shadows dark. I overdid the tonal contrast, and there was an imbalance of tone between the copper beech with its shadow, and the trees on the island on the right.

warmed with a touch of brown or red. The darker
tone should hide the edges of the first wash.

Adding highlights

When all the tones are balanced and agreeable,
I stand back to look at the painting. Is there an
adequate visual centre of focus? Is it sufficiently
punchy? Is the composition as a whole too bland?
This stage can be most satisfying: darkening a tree
behind a building to sharpen it or bring it forward,
adding a darker tree trunk or branch to break up a
bland stand of trees; adding a cloud to fill in an
empty space in the sky. Some highlighting can be
achieved by scratching out – the edge of a building
or roof catching the light, a forgotten halo or
crescent around the head of a figure painted
against the light.

I am conscious of the fact that these rescue
tactics are easily identifiable by experienced
watercolourists or art critics. I do it less frequently
as I climb the learning curve, and take some
comfort from the fact that Turner and other great
watercolourists were highly adept at scratching out!

△ **ORIGINAL PAINTING**
△ **ORIGINAL PAINTING**
Looking at this Cotswolds' scene again recently, I felt uncomfortable with three sections in it. The trees in front of and to the right of Burford Church were too dark and there was a muddle in the roofs of the nearest pair of cottages on the right. Finally, the lower sky on the right seemed empty.

▽ **FINISHED PAINTING**
Burford Church, Cotswolds
Watercolour
30 × 46 cm (12 × 18 in)
I tackled the sky first: after gently wetting the area, I extended the thin reddish-grey cloud across the spire. Then I added cobalt blue above the spire, a **bluish**-grey patch to the right **of** it, and a wash of raw sienna between the church and foreground tree on the right. Next, with four cycles of careful wash and mop, I lightened the dark green trees by half. For the cottages, I redefined the shadow side of the grey slate roof. Finally, using my pointed craft blade, I scratched a horizontal line behind the two chimneys. This separated the chimney shadows from the tree behind, and re-established the roofline more clearly.

Reviewing compositions

If you are dissatisfied with a finished composition, or it does not look quite right, look at it through your viewfinder. Try framing the picture in a more compact format, in every possible position. I have rescued innumerable paintings by cropping out unnecessary, distracting or unsatisfactory sections, and finding fresh, better focused, nicely balanced compositions. This is one of the simplest and least painful rescue techniques I know.

Rescue techniques

To wash out use a clean brush, large enough to provide an even wash of clean water; brush water on as lightly as possible, without removing paint, and cover the selected area precisely. Lift colour by

△ ORIGINAL PAINTING
This lovely hill town beside Lake Bracciano was painted swiftly in the fading light of late afternoon. When I got home, it looked insipid and flat. There was a lot wrong with it, but it boiled down simply to a lack of tonal contrast and insufficient recession.

△ FINISHED PAINTING
Bracciano, near Rome
Watercolour
24 × 34 cm (9 ½ × 13 ½ in)
First I darkened the greens around the foreground white house, and the hedge sloping down across the field.

I enhanced the blue-green trees in the middle distance, and also the brown bank in front of the house. The tone of the foreground shadow was warmed up with green-brown. The two roofs in the middle of the picture received an extra layer of burnt sienna. Finally, I washed out about a third of the colour of the castle and church, and laid over them a dilute wash of cobalt blue. I think the picture has come alive, and there is now a better sense of recession.

△ **ORIGINAL PAINTING**
I was pleased to capture the hazy late afternoon light on this ancient village overlooking Lake Bracciano. But the monotonous shoreline across the picture bothered me.

△ **VISUAL FOCUS**
I decided to break the shoreline up with a sailing boat. I drew the outline of the boat on watercolour paper and cut away the shape with a tiny pair of nail scissors to avoid jagged edges. Placing the paper template in position, I sponged and mopped out the paint within the shape; I could remove only about 70 per cent of it.

△ **FINISHED PAINTING**
Anguillara, near Rome
Watercolour
28 × 38 cm (11 × 15 in)
Because the boat and sail were appropriately grey they did not compete with the sharp reflection of the sun on the water. Some pigments, such as Winsor blue or alizarin crimson, may be more difficult to sponge out; HP paper is easier than Rough, and surface-sized paper gets a different result from internally sized paper. Avoid uneven or ragged edges when cutting out the shape. Should the paper template be too thick or too thin, or held down unevenly during sponging, water will seep under the edges. Practise first.

the mopping process and not by scrubbing with the brush. I use a ball of ordinary soft tissue paper. Lift the colour a little at a time, in stages, until the appropriate amount has been removed.

Darkening: there should be no difficulty in applying another coat of the same colour. Beware mixes of opaque pigments: a double layer of such mixes may turn dull or muddy. Remember that mixing the three primary colours together makes dark grey. I sometimes prefer to glaze with dilute French ultramarine or cobalt blue to darken cloud shadows, trees or foliage.

Scratch out with a sharp pointed craft knife, especially on heavyweight paper. Some surface-sized papers are more tenacious, but gentle persistence will eventually work, unless the tip of the blade is blunt. Avoid piercing the paper.

△ ORIGINAL PAINTING
I enjoyed painting this view, but when I stood back, I felt that it was too busy with too many trees of different colours, and scattered rocks. Even the top half of the sky was rather fussy. The bridge was too light-toned and was overwhelmed by the trees, but if I warmed it up, it would compete with the figure as the centre of focus.

△ FINISHED PAINTING
Bridge to Seathwaite, Cumbria
Watercolour
30 × 46 cm (12 × 18 in)
I decided that cropping made the composition more crisp and harmonious. The trees were more uniform in tone, most of the rocks were gone, and the sky was less busy. The figure remained the centre of focus, and the bridge became a more distinct feature.

◁ **ORIGINAL PAINTING**
The variety of boats and their colours and shapes inspired this painting. But there was rather a lot of dull grey sky, and a band of grey-green trees in the background of the picture. The white foreground boat pulled the eye down and unbalanced the composition.

△ **FINISHED PAINTING**
The White Anchor,
Pinmill, Suffolk
Watercolour
36 × 51 cm (14 × 20 in)
By cropping out most of the sky, the main masts and half the white boat in the foreground, the composition became better balanced, with the help of the red buoy on the right. The viewer could enjoy the boats without distraction or the eye being drawn out of the picture on the lower left.

12 A fresh eye

GERALD GREEN

Paintings that have lost their impact can be re-evaluated and reworked in order to reignite your first excitement with a subject.

As a creative activity, painting can never be about certainties. Although experience can point us in the right direction, however accomplished we might be there will always be times when things don't work out as we might want. This does not always mean that problematical paintings have to be discarded, since there may well be ways of rescuing them.

Deciding on solutions is made easier when looking at a painting with a fresh eye. Putting it away for two or three weeks before making any changes enables you to make a more objective re-evaluation. Looking at a painting upside-down or in a mirror helps you see any irregularities in the drawing or composition.

△ ORIGINAL PAINTING
Outdoor Café, Portofino, Italy
45 × 60 cm (18 × 24 in)
The general tonal patterns are what attracted me to this subject. When I re-evaluated the painting, it lacked a well-defined centre of interest.

The most effective way to avoid encountering problems is by being well prepared from the outset. It helps to be clear about the 'what', 'why' and 'how' for any painting before you start: what is to be your subject; why did you respond to it in the way you did and how do you intend to present it? There are ways to rectify the difficulties that can occur within each of these areas.

Subject matter

Whatever your preference, subjects are always more interesting when they consist of contrasting forms, with varieties of patterns and textures, and when they have a clearly defined centre of interest. What can often lead paintings into difficulties is the tendency to include too much in them. Producing preliminary sketches, even when painting on the spot, can help you determine exactly what is going to be the focus in a picture and, just as importantly, what can then be left out altogether.

It is worth bearing in mind that something which at first glance appears to be an interesting subject may not always translate into an appealing painting. So the drawing process should be used as a means of exploring the chosen subject to determine where its true potential might lie. This also helps you to see beyond the more obvious or picturesque features towards something which may evoke a greater personal response to whatever it was about the subject that caught your eye in the first place.

Even with these preparatory steps in place things can still go wrong. In *Outdoor Café, Portofino, Italy* (left), I had been through the preliminary stages and it was not until I had completed the painting that it seemed to be too busy. Since I felt this was a problem in the overall composition, I thought the most effective solution would be to try cropping the image in order to create a more defined focus.

Using two L-shaped pieces of mountboard as a viewfinder, I tried several different compositions. The second painting, *Outdoor Café, Portofino, Italy* (below), shows my final choice. By taking out the less prominent of the two figure groups, the remaining single group then became a more dominant feature, which gave the painting greater clarity.

Sometimes just one small part of a problematical painting can be used in this way, so you do have to be ruthless and discard anything that is superfluous.

Response to a subject

To be clear about what you want to portray in a painting, you must be certain about exactly what it was about the subject that attracted you to it in the first place. This might be light, pattern, weather, mood, or perhaps a message or statement about something in the subject itself. Painting a particular scene or object because it is 'beautiful' or because you feel it will make a 'nice picture', are such fuzzy notions that they tend to generate equally vague pictorial responses.

▽ **FINISHED PAINTING**
Outdoor Café, Portofino, Italy
Oil on board
37 × 45 cm (16 × 18 in)
This is my final version of the painting that has been cropped down to improve the composition.

What had initially attracted me to the subject of the original painting *Flowers on a Window Sill* (right) was the beautiful pattern of the flowers set against the light coming in from the window behind them. Although I felt at this stage that the painting caught the essence of the subject, when I looked at it again after a couple of weeks, it appeared weak and wishy-washy.

Often such problems are caused by an ineffective distribution of tonal values (lights and darks) and I felt this was the main problem here. The close

△ ORIGINAL PAINTING
I felt that this painting caught the essence of the subject, but that the colours seemed rather pale and bland.

◁ FINISHED PAINTING
Flowers on a Window Sill
Watercolour on 640 gsm
Rough Arches paper
35 × 52 cm (14 × 21 in)
I applied a second darker wash of the original colour over the entire background, carefully working around the flowers, jar and leaves to create more defined contrasts. This had the effect of enlivening the whole painting.

tonal proximity between the flowers and the background was not pronounced enough to make them stand out. If you look at the original painting closely, it is clear that the composition was made up of predominantly lighter tones with a few really strong dark areas. I felt this was unsatisfactory and thought about ways to improve the painting.

I felt that this could be remedied by darkening the overall tone of the background, so I applied a wash of the same colour I had used initially, working around the shape of the flowers, leaves and jar. Now, compared with the first stage, the flowers in the revised painting (above), appear to be more defined, making the whole painting a much more powerful statement.

Presentation

Sticking to the familiar, well-tried and tested methods of presentation might seem to be the best way to avoid things going wrong during the painting process. However, since each new painting presents a different set of circumstances, what worked for you previously may not be the appropriate course of action in every case, so it is inevitable that you will have to try out different approaches. In the long term, this adds to your experience, even if more immediately it increases the chances of encountering problems.

What had initially attracted me to the subject in *Pavement Café Montmartre, Paris*, First version (above right) was the way in which the light created broad patterns of tonal contrast between the shaded foreground and lighter background features, and in particular the way it caught the edges of some elements in the middle distance.

Even though my approach to the painting was similar to the manner in which I had undertaken others, I realized as I painted that I had lost sight of my original response, and the final result did not convey my original intentions. Looking at the painting in a mirror it appeared cluttered, lacking a definite centre of interest, and the colours I had used, chosen to resemble those of the subject itself now appeared rather dull and lifeless.

Simplification

In cases like this, where there appear to be problems with much of the painting, simplification can often be the way forward. I decided that I needed to disentangle the foreground and background elements by increasing the tonal contrast between them. I also thought that cropping the image from the left would improve the composition and that the whole thing could be simplified further by using a reduced colour palette. In this way I hoped to rescue the painting, even this meant virtually repainting the entire picture.

Pavement Café, Montmartre, Paris, Second version (right) shows my revised painting. Although it was an improvement, I felt that the foreground activity still dominated the image too much, so I decided to reduce the content again by taking out most of the foreground figures. *Pavement Café, Montmartre, Paris* (see page 74), shows my final composition. This now places the centre of interest firmly in the middle distance and captures the essence of what had first caught my eye in the subject. By understating the foreground features and enlivening the colour passages I was able to further invigorate the painting.

Often even well-thought-out paintings can require several stages of reworking before they reach a state of completion. Unless you keep hold of your original response to your subject it is very easy to lose your way during the painting process, with the result that you can sometimes end up painting several pictures in one painting, making your pictures appear confused or over-laboured.

△ FIRST VERSION
45 × 60 cm (18 × 24 in)
I thought I had resolved my approach to the subject in this painting, but it appeared to lack impact.

▽ SECOND VERSION
45 × 35 cm (18 × 14 in)
I cropped the image from the left to improve the composition and repainted it with a reduced colour palette while redefining the tonal contrasts. It still did not catch my initial response, so I decided that it needed further simplification.

△ **FINISHED PAINTING**
Pavement Café,
Montmartre, Paris
45 × 35 cm (18 × 14 in)
To emphasize the light in the
middle distance I took out

most of the remaining figures
and repainted the foreground,
understating the features. This
made the painting a simpler
statement and was closer to my
first impression of the scene.

13 In reflective mood

RAY BALKWILL

The artist transformed a discarded watercolour of a harbour scene using pastels to enhance contrasts of colour and tone.

The production of a successful painting rests on a number of factors, such as composition, contrast and colour. When it comes to contrast and colour, watercolours need much more forward planning than other media in order to succeed. Happily, though, rescuing an unsatisfactory painting can sometimes be a very simple matter. For example, with the aid of a couple of L-shaped pieces of mountboard, the picture can often be cropped to make the composition work more successfully.

△ **SKETCH**
Polperro Harbour
Charcoal and felt-tip pen
25.5 × 33 cm (10 × 13 in)
Although I had taken some photographs for reference, I preferred to refer to my charcoal sketch throughout. Seeing the scene in terms of shapes and varying tones not only simplified the busy harbour scene, but also determined the compositional priorities more easily.

▷ **ORIGINAL PAINTING**
Polperro Harbour
Watercolour
35.5 × 43 cm (14 × 17 in)

One of my favourite haunts is Polperro in Cornwall and I find there is nothing more exciting than sketching or painting the activities in the bustling harbour. However, I was dissatisfied with this particular watercolour and had consigned it to a drawer for about a year. When I came across it I realized that it could be successfully rescued.

The original painting

A careful assessment of the colours and tones suggested that the painting was rather bland, lacking contrast and atmosphere. Despite this, I felt that the composition was successful overall, particularly as I had cropped the fishing boat on the right in order to focus on the dark yacht as my centre of interest.

It was the reflections in the water and the patterns in the wet mud that formed my initial response to the scene; this was the essence of the

△ STAGE ONE
I chose pale colours to complement those already used in the watercolour.

△ STAGE TWO
Softening the newly applied pastels conveys the impression of trees and buildings in the background.

painting and it was this important ingredient that I had to pick up again and retain.

Nevertheless, some important decisions still had to be made before attempting to rescue the painting. Firstly, I had to decide whether to continue in watercolour or add pastel. There is always the risk that by adding further watercolour washes, the painting could lose its transparency and become overworked.

Painting with watercolour and pastel combined has been my main interest for some years now. Ideally, I prefer to start out with the clear intention of combining the two media from the outset. The transparency of watercolour and the opacity and vibrancy of pastel work extremely well together and their interplay produces paintings that are rich in a variety of marks, colour and technique. Perhaps this would be the perfect solution if this painting were to succeed?

By combining the two media and bringing together a number of different techniques, the mood, contrast and tone could be greatly enhanced to create a livelier and more balanced painting. I feel that in the finished painting this has resulted in a more honest representation of the atmosphere to be found in this picturesque harbour.

In rescuing a painting you need to work quickly and be prepared to take risks.

Stage one

I began by applying broad areas of soft pastel used on its side, with a combination of cool greens, greys and purples to further enhance the recession of the scene and create a stronger plane for the background. The light pressure applied over the tooth of the paper gave me the effect of broken colour and allowed the watercolour beneath to show through. This is very effective when using contrasting or complementary colours. Here, though, I decided on a limited palette of related colours similar to those already used in the watercolour stage in order to maintain an overall harmony.

Stage two

Using a tissue, I softened some of the pastel to make some tonal adjustments between the

△ STAGE THREE
Darkening this area has
defined the fishing boats and
given a sense of the texture
of the wall.

△ STAGE FOUR
This stage made each fishing
boat distinct from the other.

▷ ASSESSMENT STAGE
The painting was now more
balanced and just awaiting the
finishing touches.

passages of blended pastel and the areas of broken
colour. It was important to keep the background as
simple and suggestive as possible. The last thing
I needed here was detail, as it was an impression of
buildings and trees that I needed to convey.

Stage three

The middle distance with the harbour wall and
building was not working and needed to be
darkened to bring it forward more and also help to
define the two fishing boats. I lightly applied dark
green, cool green and brown ochre pastels to
achieve the correct tonal value, as well as suggest
the texture of the stone wall. The dark green pastel
was also carried down into the water to suggest the
reflection at the same time.

Stage four

The fishing boats were undifferentiated, so I added
further detail by using the purple grey pastel
already used in the background as well as further
painting with watercolour using a small round
brush. For this I used a purplish mix of cerulean
and permanent rose. I also added stronger colour
using a dark red-brown pastel on the hulls of the
boats and in the reflection.

Assessment stage

At this assessment stage, I felt that the basic
structure of the painting was far more balanced by

△ STAGE FIVE
The combination of
watercolour and pastel worked
well to portray the water.

△ STAGE SIX
The addition of some purple
grey pastel enhanced the
reflection of the boat, and
made it more true to life.

▷ USING A MOUNT
Assessing small areas within
a painting can be useful to see
if they work or not. Placing a
small mount over parts of the
foreground confirmed to me
that it already 'read' as wet
mud, so this area was best
left alone.

the adjustment of contrast and colour. The centre
of interest was where I had left the strongest
contrast of light and dark; this was the yacht on
the left, which had not been touched. All that was
required now were the finishing touches. When
working with pastels it is important to maintain a
unity within the painting, so it is worth looking to
see where else you can use a colour while it is still
in your hand. Note, for instance, how I repeated the
cool green used in the background for the seaweed
in the foreground mud.

Stage five

The transparency and fluidity of watercolour is the
perfect medium for portraying water, which is often
best represented as simply as possibly. However,
blending pastel with a finger or a tissue can also be
effective. Here, though, I decided to paint back into
the pastel with a medium round brush and water to
soften the pastel still further. I also added a light
and dark brown-pink pastel to the foreground to
help guide the eye into the painting.

Stage six

Reflections always fascinate me and it was this that
was my initial response to the scene, so they were
an important element in the picture. The general
rule is that dark reflects lighter and light reflects
darker. I felt this was working but to be accurate
I added a purple grey pastel in the reflection of the
boat. Further detail was also added to the quayside
building using a dark purple pastel.

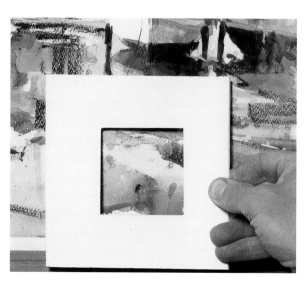

△ STAGE SEVEN
I included the figure to draw
the eye further
into the picture
and to give a
sense of scale.

△ STAGE EIGHT
The highlight here helps to
separate the building from the
background.

Stage seven

Even though the focal point of the painting was
the yacht on the left, I decided to include a figure
in the scene to help draw the eye still further into
the picture. This was put in with a mixture of
watercolour and gouache, using a reference in my
sketchbook. The introduction of a figure in a
painting suggests a narrative element as well as
providing a sense of scale, and can often bring a
scene to life.

Stage eight

Using a small round brush and resting the ferrule
on a plastic ruler I gently glided the brush along
to put in the highlight on the top of the roof
with white gouache. This helped to separate the
building from the background. I also added a
brown-ochre pastel to the roofs echoing the
underlying watercolour stage.

△ RIGGING AND ROPES
To make sure that these
elements were not overdone,
I used a 4B graphite pencil
rather than a brush.

Spattering is useful for creating texture. Making sure that I had first masked the rest of the painting with a piece of scrap paper, I flicked some paint into the foreground using a medium round brush and watercolour. I also added a few touches of light blue pastel in the mud and around the dark yacht. Foregrounds should be kept simple.

▷ **SPATTERING**
By using this technique I was able to add more texture to the piece.

△ **FINISHED PAINTING**
Polperro Harbour
Mixed media
33.5 × 43 cm (14 × 17 in)

14 Subjects for change

OLWEN TARRANT

With the addition of a pattern motif, a figure and objects, the artist solved the problems posed by three unsatisfactory paintings.

Many artists admit when they have finished a painting that something, somewhere is not quite right, not quite what they intended, or perhaps they have overworked the painting and lost its sparkle, and its originality. Knowing when a painting is finished can be an extremely difficult decision to make, especially when that decision has to be made by the artist personally. The painter knows what was intended; the rest of the world may not. The artist may go on deceiving himself or herself that it is a faultless masterpiece: the rest of the world will not.

I believe that one of the strongest principles in art is to be honest with oneself, even if it means the risk of destroying the work. Many of the great artists, as we all know, spent hours either starting again or making radical changes.

We know that sometimes a painting falls below what we intended. To be faced with problems is one of the greatest attractions and challenges of becoming an artist. Whether they can be solved to one's own satisfaction is life on another plane; sometimes one feels like throwing the painting on the nearest rubbish tip.

But before taking this drastic step, I feel it is wise to take the painting into a different environment, perhaps hanging it on a living room wall, and looking at it casually now and again. What appears to be wrong with a painting can suddenly hit me at the most unexpected time and I can, hopefully, put it right. The three examples tackled here came readily to mind; there have been many more.

The problems posed by these three paintings were solved by the addition of a pattern motif, a figure and objects. The opposite, that is, the removal of certain aspects, could equally be the case in other paintings. What is important is to stand back, admit that there is something not quite right, and look at it in a different environment. It is never easy.

Costume drama

I did the painting *Destiny and the Dream* (below) directly from my imagination without any outside source material. All too easily I can become totally involved with particular aspects of the work in the cocooned atmosphere of my studio, so I hung it in my sitting room where it remained for some time.

The figures in the painting are performers, and it occurred to me that they should be attired in attractive costumes. Any added colours, however,

△ **ORIGINAL PAINTING**
This painting was done directly from my imagination without any outside source material.

Destiny and the Dream
Oil on canvas
76 × 76 cm (30 × 30 in)

It occurred to me that the performers should be dressed in attractive costumes. Bearing in mind that any pattern should not conflict with the other shapes, I changed the plain costume of the male figure to a harlequin design.

had to be totally sympathetic to the whole of the painting. Any pattern motif must not conflict with the other shapes in the work.

My palette was French ultramarine, cadmium red, alizarin crimson, viridian, Indian yellow and titanium white. Staying with those colour hues, I changed the plain costume of the male figure to a strong harlequin design. I could see that the painting was coming to life but I needed to work all over the picture plane enhancing other colours to a similar strength of colour hue and tone. I enhanced the tone of the dress of the female figure and added more yellow to the white mix for the daisies to make them stand out from the dress. The colour hue of the dress was automatically strengthened by the red and green costume of the male.

Tranquil Figure

The Rocking Chair (right) was painted out of doors on site in Spain, and the intimacy of the partly

shaded courtyard was what originally appealed to me. However, when I looked at the finished painting back in my studio, it did not convey the real feeling of being in that courtyard. In the painting the courtyard appeared tranquil, but there was someone there: I was there. I was an intruder. It needed a human being to emphasize the intimacy and tranquillity. The woman in the rocking chair was stored in my memory from the many older Spanish women I had seen sitting quietly sewing or shelling nuts.

In adding a figure to a painting it is wise first to establish the scale of the figure and put a couple of marks at the top and bottom of the space as a guide. It is important to stay within the range of the original palette of colours (Winsor blue, cadmium red, Indian yellow, alizarin crimson and titanium white).

Another problem was that there seemed in my memory to be more foliage enclosing the courtyard than I had shown. I use camera shots as a useful

◁ **ORIGINAL PAINTING**
This partly shaded Spanish courtyard was what originally inspired me. However, my painting did not convey the real feeling of being there. It was lacking something.

▽ **FINISHED PAINTING**
The Rocking Chair
Oil on canvas
61 × 76 cm (24 × 30 in)
The addition of the woman in the rocking chair, sewing, emphasized the intimacy and tranquillity of the courtyard.

reference and in this case I referred to them to look for the kind of foliage that would match the strong curving shapes of the painting. The ferns were perfect for this and I mixed a strong green with Winsor blue, Indian yellow and titanium white to establish the ferns in the foreground. I scumbled alizarin crimson through the shadow areas to give more depth. The fabric being worked on by the woman is the brightest tone of the painting and leads the eye to the figure.

▷ ORIGINAL PAINTING
To give the feeling of strong sunlight flooding in, the canvas was covered with a yellow ground colour. But studying it away from the scene I was unhappy with it. I hung it up in the dining room where it remained for some time.

Foreground Interest

When I first worked on *The Mandalay Jug* (above), I thought of this scene as a field of shapes and colours. My palette for this painting was cadmium red, cadmium yellow, viridian, alizarin crimson, French ultramarine and titanium white. Initially I had covered the canvas with a yellow ground colour to give the feeling of strong sunlight through the window, but looking at it away from the scene I was dissatisfied with it and hung it on the wall in the dining room.

It was much later that I felt something was needed to take the eye into the painting. I wandered around the house and a Mandalay jug seemed to be the perfect object to complement the colours and shapes of that particular painting. I placed it so that the curve of the handle echoed the curves of the backs of the chairs and added a further curve with a bowl of fruit, keeping the fruit a similar colour to the flowers. I made the white background colour of the jug a slightly lower tone than the white walls of the house opposite so that, while I had created more interest in the foreground, the viewer's eye would follow through the window to the cottage.

I mixed French ultramarine with cadmium red for the very dark blue of the pattern on the jug and I introduced some transparent gold ochre with French ultramarine and a little alizarin crimson for the basic white of the jug, while using the stronger cadmium yellow when mixing the white of the cottage walls.

△ FINISHED PAINTING
The Mandalay Jug
Oil on canvas
76 × 76 cm (30 × 30 in)
After a while I realized that
something was needed to
draw the eye into the painting.
The Mandalay jug seemed to
be an ideal object to
complement the colours and
shapes of this painting.

The painting plan

JOHN MITCHELL

Following a structured strategy – from initial inspiration to final brushstroke – will help you to avoid disappointing results and painting disasters.

What makes a painting look right? Is a painting ever finished, and how do we know if it is? How can we give ourselves the best chance of producing a successful work? I suppose it is a subjective decision to say that a painting looks 'right'. However, formal elements also come into play. For example, the drawing may look wrong, the colour incorrect, the tone unhappy. These qualities must be considered in advance to give ourselves the best chance of getting them 'right'. However, changes may also have to be made while producing the painting, to rescue it or restore the original vision that we had in our mind's eye.

Is a painting ever finished? Well, yes and no. Have you ever had the experience of completing a picture quickly, and getting it framed and sent off to exhibition? When you see it hanging you realize that there is something wrong with the colour or composition. On reflection perhaps it would have been better not to show it so quickly. Wasn't it Cézanne who would leave a painting on view in his studio for months or even a year or two until one day he would find exactly the right colour with which to finish it? A painting, like fine wine,

needs time to mature. Let's change the question: is a given subject ever finished? Not necessarily so, I believe.

I have taken one of my favourite subjects and repainted it to demonstrate how best to prepare for producing a painting and what changes might occur along the way. The subject is an area in Skye called Coire na Creiche, the Corrie of the Spoils, at the entrance to Glen Brittle. There is a delightful river in the bed of the corrie with beautiful pools and waterfalls, the 'Fairy Pools'. The corrie is dominated by a triangular mountain, Sgurr an Fheadain, with a distinct cleft from top to bottom. Why does this subject fascinate me? It's a combination of the dramatic setting, the formal elements of the mountain, rocks and pool, and memories of times spent in the corrie on my own and with different people.

Developing the painting

The first tactic in developing a painting is to explore the subject with sketches and photographs made on the spot. This information is taken into the studio and developed in drawings and thumbnail sketches. You can try using different media, perhaps new to you. Explore the possibilities of unusual compositions, for example extended landscape or portrait shapes. Draw in pen and ink or wash. Use different colour schemes. Really get inside your subject.

You might feel that this will dull interest in the subject and produce a tired painting. One of my college tutors, John Maxwell, told me that a painting is a combination of the initial aesthetic impulse combined with strong formal elements developed through sketches. Of course, the

▷ **PHOTOGRAPHIC REFERENCE**
This photograph shows Fairy Pool with Sgurr an Fheadain in the background. It is a spectacular place and there is a good path well into the corrie.

△ **FIRST PAINTING**
I had painted Coire na Creiche
before. Some subjects are
worth repeating and exploring.

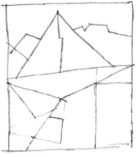

△ **COMPOSITION SKETCHES**
These sketches done in
water-soluble pencil are
useful for trying out different
arrangements of the basic
composition. Time spent on
these is never wasted even if
you end up going back to your
first idea.

◁ **PEN AND INK
ILLUSTRATION**
Coire na Creiche
13.5 × 11 cm (5 ¼ × 4 ¼ in)
This drawing was made for
the Scottish Mountaineering
Club Journal. Before going on
to do paintings I like to
explore the theme in different
media, familiarizing myself
with the subject.

△ **COLOUR SKETCHES**
13 × 8.5 cm (5 × 3 ½ in)
In these gouache sketches
different colour schemes were
tried out. These are very useful
and allow the main painting
to be approached with more
confidence as the main
colour plan has been worked
out in advance.

difficulty lies in the combination. But it really is
worthwhile giving this method a chance.

As the painting develops it will gain momentum
and make its own demands. Changes in even the
best worked-out scheme will have to be made. One
important reason is that often sketches will be on a
small scale and the final work on a larger one. Keep
an open mind about how the painting develops:
this is the second tactic for success.

The third tactic is to try to surprise yourself.
Look at your painting in a mirror, turn it upside-
down on the easel, use larger brushes, experiment
with textures (often neglected), try glazing colours,
and examine it through half-closed eyes. Aim to
develop a technical and practical repertoire and use
it appropriately.

The fourth tactic is to be prepared to put the
painting aside for a few days and return to it with
a fresh eye. You will immediately become aware of
changes that should be made.

A subject can be developed into a series of
paintings. One version might focus on colour,

fine pumice gel

coarse pumice gel

fine moulding paste

◁ **TEXTURE EXPERIMENTS**
A main part of the painting
will comprise of rock surfaces.
Exercises such as these in
acrylic gels and pastes are an
opportunity to try out different
textures before committing to
the final work. Better to make
mistakes on these than on the
final work!

texture paste

gold mica flake

silver mica flake

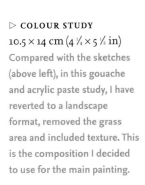

▷ **COLOUR STUDY**
10.5 × 14 cm (4 ¼ × 5 ½ in)
Compared with the sketches
(above left), in this gouache
and acrylic paste study, I have
reverted to a landscape
format, removed the grass
area and included texture. This
is the composition I decided
to use for the main painting.

△ **WORKING SKETCH**
13.5 × 18 cm (5 ¼ × 7 in)
I enlarged the colour study
on page 89 using a scanner,
and then drew guidelines over
the print to help me enlarge
the sketch on to the painting
board. The final board or
canvas must be the same
proportion as the sketch.

another on light and shade, and yet another on texture. Think of Monet's haystacks or lily ponds. So while you are working on one painting make mental or actual notes of how you might make another version. Accept the unexpected and surprise yourself.

If there appears to be something wrong with your picture and you can't quite think what it is, try looking at each formal element in turn. Is the drawing bad, or is the colour the problem? If you are uncertain about one area, try standing back and extending your arm so that your thumb covers the offending fragment of the painting. Does that look better or worse?

If one area dominates the picture, try to devise methods of getting your eye to move round the canvas. Maybe colour could be used, maybe texture, or tonal effects. If, on the other hand, the painting looks a bit flat overall, then you should develop a centre of interest where the eye can rest briefly before moving on.

There is more to making a painting than colouring in a drawing made on to a board or canvas. Painting is a blend of intellectual and practical activities. Of course, there will always be some paintings that seem to paint themselves but I am convinced that they are the result of careful preparation.

◁ FIRST DRAWING
A drawing on to the board, which has been toned with burnt umber acrylic paint on top of two layers of white acrylic gesso. Here you can see traces of the enlarging process. The initial drawing was done in charcoal but in the upper half I have started to redraw in blue paint, adjusting the drawing as a I go along.

◁ FINISHED DRAWING
The drawing has been finished and the sky painted in.

Now the crunch question: how do you know if a painting is finished? There is no right or wrong answer but there are some guidelines. As soon as you think it is finished, put it aside for a few days so that you can come back to it with a fresh eye. Ask a friend whose opinion you value to have a look at it. And, last but by no means least, trust to instinct. Don't be in a rush to get a painting finished: a good painting needs time to come to fruition.

▷ **PAINTING STAGE ONE**
Rough colour and tones are
now painted. At this stage, you
need to pay attention to tone,
which is the skeleton of the
painting that you will later
clothe with colour.

△ **PAINTING STAGE TWO**
A lot of work has been done
on the mountains, with subtler
colours and tones. Textures
have been introduced into the
rock areas using acrylic gels
and pastes.

Tips for success

Get to know your subject intimately and do as
much preparatory work as possible. Do not focus
too much work on one small area of the painting.
Take an overall view and keep the whole picture
going at the same time. If a particular colour looks
'wrong', try using its complementary. Try working
to a time scale, and stick to it. Find out how other
artists have treated a similar theme. If it has all
gone horribly 'wrong', destroy it and start again.

Always bear in mind what originally attracted
you to the subject? Try to recapture that feeling in
the painting. Don't be afraid to discard a favourite
part of your painting, painting over it if necessary
for the overall effect. Enjoy yourself, and let
enjoyment show in your work.

△ **FINISHED PAINTING**
Coire na Creiche
Acrylic on board
44 × 60 cm (17 ½ × 23 ¼ in)
Final adjustments have been
made to the mountains. A lot
of work has been done on the
rock areas with textures and
glazes developed, dry paint
dragged over contrasting
colours and the bottom-right
corner calmed down. Small
patches of strong colour
have been added as has a
suggestion of vegetation
among the rocks.

16 No contest

HUGO GRENVILLE

By charting the progess of a painting, the artist shows how he changed the composition to remove elements that were 'fighting each other'.

Over the past 25 years of picture making I have become aware that there is often an uncomfortable shortfall betweeen the vision of my idea for a painting, and the results of its execution. The very canvas seems to have a life of its own, and even the brushes seem ill-tempered towards my grand intentions. This discrepancy between what I set out to achieve and what I am capable of delivering used to worry me all the time until I slowly realized that my approach was flawed, and that the point of painting a subject was to explore it, to unravel it in paint and to make discoveries. The process has to be revelatory, not confirmatory, and this entails making changes as the picture progresses. Some of these changes might need to be substantial (such as altering a central part of the design) and some might simply be refinements, but whatever they are they should be seen as a positive part of the process, indeed even as the *sine qua non* of flexibility and open-mindedness. Once I absorbed the implications of this new approach I found a much greater sense of freedom in painting, and have enormously enjoyed the sense of discovery that accompanies each journey into paint.

▷ **STAGE ONE**
My first concern was how the space should be divided up. Here the model is too far to the right of the picture.

◁ STAGE TWO

Next, I reduced the size of the
figure and moved her into a
more central position. I felt
that this was the right shape
and it became clearer how
to resolve the rest of the
composition.

Stage one

I had already completed an earlier version of
this subject and decided to explore it further by
incorporating a little more of the space around the
figure. The first major concern was where exactly
I should place the figure in the context of the
canvas: in other words, how the pictorial space
should be divided up. My first attempt was
awkward and, as you can see, resulted in the figure
being too far to the right of the canvas.

Stage two

At the next session with Yvette, my model, I decided
to reduce the scale of the figure and move her more
into the centre of the canvas. Having established
what felt like the right key shape, it gradually
became easier to resolve the remainder of the
composition. I began to indicate the darker areas
within the room, and the beginning of the patterns
on the sofa fabric with broad washes of violet grey
and rose madder.

▷ **STAGE THREE**

I introduced the pattern of the rug on the floor, and the rough shape of the flowers behind the figure's head, although I was not sure whether I wanted to keep these flowers.

◁ **STAGE FOUR**

At this stage the painting was getting too hot, so I used ultramarine blue to cool it down and accentuated the dark areas to heighten the tonal range. However, after reviewing the whole canvas, I was still unhappy with several elements.

◁ **FINISHED PAINTING**
Kneeling Nude
Oil on canvas
76 × 81.2 cm (30 × 32 in)
After removing the easel
and the jug, repainting
and softening the flowers,
harmonizing the blues and
greys and introducing the
books on the rug, I reviewed
the changes. I was pleased
to see that the individual
elements were no longer
fighting each other.

Stage three

I continued to define the shapes of objects around the figure, introducing the pattern of the rug on the floor, and the rough shape of the flowers behind Yvette's head. At this stage I was beginning to have doubts about whether I wanted these flowers at all. They began to seem too dominant.

Stage four

I felt that the painting was getting too hot, so I introduced ultramarine blue to help cool it down. The dark areas were then accentuated to heighten the tonal range, and both the figure and the space around her were further defined. As the paint became thicker I reviewed the whole canvas and came to the following conclusions: the patterns on the fabric of the screen (top left corner) were in conflict with the shape of the easel in front of it; the darks had become too dark, especially in the rug (bottom left); the blues in the sofa fabric were too bright; the flowers were too insistent, and they had lost their sense of design; the right-hand edge of the painting seemed disconnected and unsatisfactory, and needed further thought.

Finishing touches

The following week I removed the easel from the painting, along with the jug on the window sill. I repainted and softened the flowers, and tried to harmonize the blues and greys throughout the composition. I introduced the books on the rug to increase the force of the diagonal made by the figure and to create a lead-in from the bottom-left hand corner. I softened the staccato of the darks on the figure. As I stepped back to review the changes in the picture, I could see immediately that the individual elements in the composition were no longer fighting each other, and had become subordinate to an overall senses of design, which I felt, enhanced the sense of mood and emotion.

17 The feel-right factor

CAROL HODGSON

The artist had no qualms about altering the composition of two different pastels until she felt happy to carry on painting.

Many obstacles can stand in the way of a painting emerging from a blank canvas, or in my case a piece of paper. Difficulties encountered with materials or application can hamper attempts in capturing the essence of the subject. On the other hand, one can become overly concerned with the essence or concept and run the risk of overworking the painting in an attempt to achieve it.

△ PENCIL SKETCH
A rough sketch provides me with good reference material and helps me to understand the subject better.

Happy to dispose of a painting if I am having little success in achieving a desired effect or mood, I treat the early stages of the painting process as experimental. This approach means disposing of the painting should all the elements be amiss. This might seem quite drastic but if it means salvaging the inspiration at the mercy of the materials then I have no compunction in doing so. When the two connect it's wonderful but it's rare that a painting emerges without encountering some sort of technical or emotional problems along the way.

I sometimes start a painting many times over, searching for that elusive 'feel-right factor'. Here I've chosen two paintings that took different paths to completion.

Reference material

Even when using photographs for reference it's worthwhile making sketches to understand the subject better. I often find myself lapsing into a subconscious state of mind without the constraints of picturemaking, and often make many more useful discoveries about the subject.

While I was touring Stratford-upon-Avon, Warwickshire with foreign visitors a picturesque scene caught my eye. With little time to sit and sketch I resorted to photographs to record the moment. As an amateur photographer I can take a pretty picture but replicating the mood and atmosphere which attracted me to this subject in the first place was a different matter.

Development work

Back in my studio it took many trials and discarded sheets of paper on the studio floor to recapture the initial inspiration. For this attempt I chose a

◁ **STAGE ONE**
Along with several others, this attempt was, relegated to the studio floor. I was not happy with the choice of paper colour, but the main concern was that I had not captured the intimacy that first intrigued me.

favourite dark blue paper and sketched in the main shapes, sticking to the viewpoint captured in the photograph. This second stage involves blocking in the shapes in darker tones with a light pressure of the pastel stick. As this stage progresses I continually assess whether the painting is developing as I want, and regularly ask myself questions regarding composition, balance of colours, tone and mood.

Unfortunately this attempt was relegated to the studio floor. I felt I had made the wrong choice of paper colour. I chose blue to contrast with the orange brickwork but the tone was too dark and detrimentally affected the value of the colours. But my main concern was that I was not capturing the intimacy that intrigued me so much when I first saw the cottages. This became a combination of technical and emotional difficulties.

Making radical changes

On the technical side, to set a brighter key to the painting I decided to use a red paper. I also changed the format to landscape; bringing the cottages closer to the viewer suggested a feeling of intimacy. To create a sense of curiosity I partially obscured the cottages from view, inventing a full bed of towering flowers for them to hide behind. I suspected the owners were keen gardeners, but when I took the photograph the gardens were in the latter stages of what obviously once was a glorious bed of mixed planting.

△ **FINISHED PAINTING**
Stratford Terrace and
Herbaceous Border
Pastel
28 × 35.5 cm (11 × 14 in)
To set a brighter key, I decided
to use a red paper, changed
the format to landscape and
brought the cottages closer
to the viewer, suggesting a
feeling of intimacy. I invented
a bed of towering flowers and
replaced the path with vertical
marks in the foreground,
hinting at a fence.

Not much can be done to restore the flower
beds unless you are fortunate enough to be in
the possession of artistic licence, so luckily for
me I was able to replenish them with a variety of
delphiniums, verbascum and poppies in a loose,
impressionistic manner.

The path was too obvious an entrance to the
painting and it drew the viewer too quickly up to
the focal point, so I eliminated it. It was replaced
with vertical marks hinting at a fence as a 'lead in'
for the eye. Using line acted as a useful contrast to
the lively mark-making used for the flowers. All
that remained to complete the picture was to add
the final lightest values of the roof, wall, flowers
and fence, and finally pure white on the window
frames. Oh, and to avoid a colour opposites cliché,
a red and blue door.

Spectacular skies

I live in Nottinghamshire on the border of Lincolnshire and look out over the Carrs where there are huge expanses of spectacular skies. One evening I could not resist painting the remnants of a stormy day. Painting rapidly on site, initially, I was happy with the ominous effect of the cloud formation, but after a couple of weeks a fresh look at the painting, that had been tucked away in a drawer out of sight, instigated changes.

Fortunately the initial application was done rapidly and with very light pressure, leaving much of the grain of the paper exposed, which enabled me to rework the painting.

Changes to composition

A couple of coats of fixative, which were allowed to dry between coats, further restored the tooth of the surface and fixed the pigment. With tentative marks of pastel I began to suggest the necessary changes in the composition. The sky was too dominant a feature and was heavier in value than the foreground, so to facilitate further work at a later stage I shifted the horizon level slightly up the picture. The pastel strokes in the sky had plenty of movement but were a bit too vigorous, so an area to allow the viewer's eye to relax was developed towards the top right-hand quarter. I also suggested more interest in the sky with hints of colour patterns.

Bolder approach

The earlier tentative changes in the composition now gave me enough confidence in the structure to express myself with a bolder approach. Because the top section was larger than the bottom the landscape required some dynamism to balance the two spaces, therefore a patchwork of vibrating colours was added to the foreground, allowing it to compete equally with the energetic sky.

△ STAGE ONE
At first I was happy with the effect of the cloud formation, but after a couple of weeks, I took a fresh look at the painting and decided to make some changes.

▷ STAGE TWO
The sky was too dominant and was heavier in value than the foreground, so to facilitate further work at a later stage I shifted the horizon level slightly up the picture.

△ FINISHED PAINTING
Nottinghamshire Skies
Pastel
35.5 × 35.5 cm (14 × 14 in)
Once all of the compositional
choices were made, I enjoyed
the freedom of adding colour
and texture where necessary.

As a by-product the warm reds created the
illusion of coming forward, and conversely the
addition of cool blue-greens in the sky created
recession in the horizon. The cottage added the
human element and strengthened the right middle
distance, giving the effect of balancing the angled
landscape. Happy with the earlier colours in the
sky I developed them further. I then allowed myself
to become spontaneous and enjoy the freedom of
adding colour and texture as and where needed.

18 Watercolour washes

BOB RUDD

Working one step at a time and painting with no fixed ideas about the outcome, helps the artist to capture the essence of a subject.

In my painting I try to capture the spirit of the place and also something of the excitement that I felt there. But the painting has to be independent and exciting in itself. The paintings shown here are pure watercolour used as a transparent medium, and the first marks applied are usually visible in the finished picture. I work with strong colour from the beginning, so it would be difficult to change the drawing significantly, or get back to clean paper once the painting has begun. I sometimes envy the flexibility oil painters enjoy!

My starting point is not fixed; I go for a walk. I may visit an area, but at this stage everything is potentially 'up for grabs'. I may visit a building, but I have no specific angle or view in mind. I delay making any decisions. I try to see as much of the subject as possible. This gives me the space to make discoveries and maximize my ideas. It's also the inspirational stage, and I love this time when I find artistic rejuvenation. There are two main exasperations for me, however: the weather and the light can conspire to make the subject almost impossible to see. Mostly, however, I am lucky. I am also very aware of the limitations of a two-dimensional image in being able to accommodate only a tiny fraction of all that I see and feel on a large scale.

Having taken many rolls of film, I return with enthusiasm to the neutral and objective surroundings of the studio. Here I feel able to take from the subject only what I need and consider the formal painting more easily.

Keeping options open

I liked the simplicity of the scene in my painting *Boscastle* (page 104) and the rich winter colouring in the cliffs. I work in strong colour from the outset,

which means that I have something precise to relate to in subsequent work. Also, by working the painting initially in areas, my options for the yet unpainted parts are left wide open. Here, the clean yellow in the right-hand cliff could therefore be added at quite a late stage. The consequence of this approach, of course, is that I have no plan of action, apart from proceeding one bit at a time.

Sometimes I paint an area and it works out pretty well as I imagined it would at the first attempt – and at other times it most certainly doesn't. In this painting I found myself going back to the sunlit area at the top of the cliffs again and again. I wanted to make the area sparkle as if light were striking cornfields. The difficulty was that further applications of paint created the danger of

△ **STAGE ONE**
Boscastle
The first watercolour wash always looks alarmingly strong when it is first applied because it is seen against all that white paper; it will also dry lighter.

◁ STAGE TWO
Boscastle
The painting is worked on one
step at a time, with no fixed
ideas about the next stage or
the final outcome.

▽ FINISHED PAINTING
Boscastle
Watercolour
54.5 × 73.5 cm (21 ½ × 29 in)
I wanted to capture the
essence of the simplicity of
the scene and the rich winter
colouring in the cliffs. Having
made several unsatisfactory
attempts, I resorted to
washing part of the area at the
top of the cliffs back and then
painting it again: don't be
afraid to do this. I was happy
with my second attempt.

an ever-darkening result. Having made several
attempts and failed to create the desired effect
I finally resorted to washing the area back and
made a second attempt to paint it from scratch:
don't be afraid to do this. I didn't do anything
differently, but it worked at the second attempt.
The distant hills and the foreground cliff were
strengthened and just by greater contrast this area
stood out as being brighter.

Pencil sketches

Usually, I begin a painting by making drawings
from photographs. These pencil sketches are
very intuitive, almost 'automatic drawings' made
while exploring the pictorial possibilities in the
photographs. They are little more than scribbles
but, on reflection, will suggest the general thrust
of a composition, maybe the beginnings of a
tonal arrangement and even ideas about colour.

I haven't actually had consciously to make any decisions about the final painting thus far. Just by working through these drawings decisions are magically made, ideas start to emerge. A key element, even at this stage, is keeping options open and flexible.

Distancing myself from the drawings via coffee and biscuits creates a necessary detachment or breathing space. When I return, thumbing through the sketchbook can release the potential in a drawing, or at least suggest possibilities. If this does not happen then I simply repeat the process, which means more drawings, more coffee, more detachment, and more returns.

Once I have a sketch to develop, I draw on to the final paper, taking care because it is not easily changed later. I keep working, but without having yet visualized the finished picture. Initially, areas of the painting are treated individually, working from white paper and taking them as far as possible in one session. I deliberately mix naturalistically rendered passages with others that are freely interpreted and arbitrarily invented. For example, the foam in *Longships Lighthouse from Land's End* (see page 108) was naturalistically painted because I simply loved the way it looked; however, the foreground rocks were freely interpreted with passages of complete invention because I wanted to create tension and unpredictability.

I usually begin with the part of the painting that I feel most sure about. Another piece of the jigsaw is painted to go with the first, then another to complement or contrast with those, and so on. At each stage I keep an eye on the whole being created and try to respond to the needs of the painting. My aim, within the limitations of painting, is to capture something of the essence of the place, the things that particularly caught my eye and the excitement I felt.

Creating balance

At this point I invariably face chaos. To some extent the elements that I've brought to the picture are disparate, and some fusion or marriage is necessary to make a whole. All the ingredients have been thrown into the pot. The second part of the process is to balance everything: helping the eye on its

journey around the picture by making connections, emphasizing rhythms and adjusting contrasts.

In watercolour I can only adjust and modify what is already there. The difference between a painting working or not can be really small. On the other hand, I am prepared to risk losing the painting completely by doing something quite radical that might just make an improvement. I keep going until there is absolutely nothing I feel I could do to make the work stronger. It is sometimes hard to see the work objectively when I am in the middle of it. To help, I turn the

◁ **ORIGINAL PHOTOGRAPH**
Bridge of Dulsie, River Findhorn
This is one of my original photographs, giving me a broad outline of the subject but very little of the emotion I felt when I was there.

△ **STUDIO DRAWING**
Bridge of Dulsie, River Findhorn
In this drawing I am beginning to explore the pictorial possibilities.

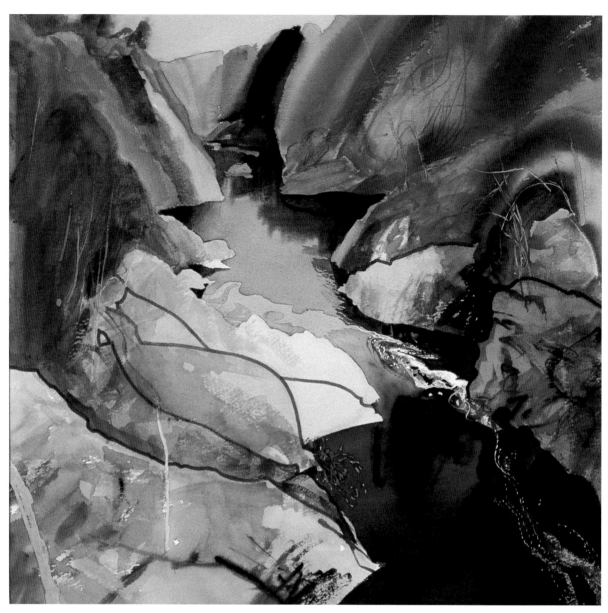

△ FINISHED PAINTING
*Bridge of Dulsie, River
Findhorn*
Watercolour
53.2 × 55.7 cm (21 × 22 in)
Here I wanted to paint the
calm, deep water with its
reflections running through
the gorge just as it was. The
problem was what to do with
the uninspiring tree detail on
each side. It was an ideal
opportunity for abstract
invention, and intuitive
painting provided the solution.

painting upside-down, or look at it reversed in a
mirror, or smaller through a reducing glass.
Viewing the painting at all stages in a working
mount or frame is essential, I find, to see it at all
clearly. Leaving it for a while, and returning with
a fresher eye also helps.

I make most of my paintings work, one way or
another, by allowing the solution to remain
unpredictable and unplanned. I never change my
mind because I never make my mind up in the
first place. Beyond this, I do face problems, and
I've tried to elaborate specifically in regard to the
three paintings shown here. Ultimately, I only
half-know what it is I am searching for, and

know it only when I find it. Even then it is surprising and not exactly what I was expecting. My advice, then, is to seize the uncertainty and enjoy the journey!

Abstract invention

In *Bridge of Dulsie, River Findhorn* (left) I knew that I wanted to paint the calm, deep water with its reflections running through the gorge very much the way it was. The problem was what to do with the rather fuzzy mass of tree detail on each side, which I found uninspiring. It was an ideal opportunity for abstract invention, and intuitive painting provided the solution. Even in free-working passages like these, there is the need to deal with a huge range of subtle contrasts: contrasts of hue, saturation, tone, hardness, softness texture etc. Gesture and feeling in the way the paint is applied are also important for me. All this complexity cannot be calculated in advance; I just have to trust my intuition and feelings, be prepared to do anything, and paint. I arrive at the solution by doing it. It often takes several goes, however, and I had to return many times to all areas because they didn't work out, apart from the clean colours at the top of the painting. My advice is to be prepared to refine, reflect and edit until you feel happy with the overall relationship being created.

Stunning view

Longships Lighthouse from Land's End was based on a stunning view from Land's End. The surf, in particular, looked amazing in a low, raking light and is probably the real subject of the picture. I wanted to capture this, but also to try to make a painting that was not entirely photographic and predictable. My sketch suggested a squarer format, with the foreground rocks piled up, that seemed to

△ **ORIGINAL PHOTOGRAPH**
Longships Lighthouse from Land's End
This photograph is an aide-mémoire for the experience of being there, as well as providing drawing reference.

◁ **SKETCHBOOK DRAWING**
Longships Lighthouse from Land's End
These drawings were referred to throughout the painting process because they suggested useful ideas.

△ **FINISHED PAINTING**
Longships Lighthouse from
Land's End
Watercolour
54.5 × 73.5 cm (21 ½ × 29 in)
Based on a stunning view
from Land's End, the surf
looked amazing in a low,
raking light and is probably
the real subject of the picture.

speak more of the drama of the place. I liked the dullish blue sea and neutral surf that I saw when I was there. The neutrals in the surf, however, turned out to be surprisingly difficult to find, and I painted the area with many washes of different pigments before I was happy.

At one stage it looked much too purple and so I washed much of it with terra verte to neutralize it. I visualized strong primary and secondary colours in the foreground and initially painted it like this. The problem I found then was in connecting the foreground with the rest of the painting. This involved a lengthy process of gradually, one step at a time, desaturating the colour until the area seemed to fit. The vibrant flashes of green and bright red that remain are hinted at in the sky.

Basic instinct

PAUL BROWN

In three diverse paintings, the artist stands back and takes time to discover what improvements can be made until he is satisfied with the end results.

My belief as to when a painting is finished is usually based on instinct. Over the last ten years I have learnt to listen to my inner voice, which not only guides me through a painting, but also tells me when to stop.

When looking at a painting after working on it, I often take a viewpoint from approximately 3 metres (10 feet) away. Immediately, I'm told what is wrong with it; what just doesn't feel right. It's a bit like hearing a duff note at a musical performance. To me an error will just stick out and be jarring on the eye. I find it is often a good idea to list the points or areas I am not happy with and then improve them. Sometimes I view the picture in a different room, or leave it until the next day. Usually I find that I can instantly see any errors in a painting as they just seem to leap out at me.

Changing the composition

I saw the image (right) on Porthminster Beach in St Ives, Cornwall by chance on a summer's day. The light in St Ives can be stunning and I was particularly taken by the colours the child and mother were wearing and also by the light and shade in the overall piece.

In the first study the two figures were sitting on a concrete walkway by the beach. There was a long shadow created by a flag and also an advertising board. In my initial painting I put all of these elements into the picture as it was what I saw. However, after the painting was about half finished I felt the composition didn't work very well. After some deliberation I decided to sketch in another figure to enhance the painting, change the composition and add some extra colour and interest. The following day I glanced at the

painting with the extra figure and realized it was a mistake and wasn't really going to work as a picture.

I had taken some other photographs around St Ives which included the sea and sky, and I felt that if I combined the two, this would enhance the composition. I set about adding in the sky and the sea and painting out the additional figure. Immediately, the painting took on a new life.

With the new composition in place I added some figures and also increased the amount of paint for the sand. I made sure that the sand area

△ **INITIAL STAGE**
Mother and Child at St Ives
At this stage there were only two figures sitting by the beach. I felt the composition didn't work very well and decided to sketch in another figure and add some extra colour and interest. When I next looked at the painting with the extra figure, I realized it was a mistake.

△ FINISHED PAINTING
Mother and Child at St Ives
Oil on canvas
45.5 × 61 cm (18 × 24 in)
I decided to add in the sky and
the sea and paint out the
additional figure. Immediately,
the painting took on a new life
and the additions gave the
composition more depth.

had more details in the foreground compared to
the background. I also painted out the advertising
board and the long shadow in the sand, and began
to build up the colour on the two figures. I changed
the colour of the sandals from alizarin crimson to
cadmium red to help make the painting sing out,
and I also changed the colour of the concrete until
I found a tone which I felt suited the overall tonal
harmony of the picture. After the initial problems,
I was very pleased with the results.

Venetian view

I saw the view of the Grand Canal on a spring day
early in the morning. The sun was just rising
and the colours along the canal were stunning.
I changed the gondola poles from blue to red and
white as this dramatically enhanced the vibrancy of
the work. This painting had taken ages to get to the
first stage, and I was still unhappy with it. I had
developed the painting using the broken brush
stroke technique in order to capture the light

◁ INITIAL STAGE
Impression along the Grand Canal, Venice
This painting was developed using the broken brush stroke technique in order to capture the light effects, but in the process I wasn't happy with the buildings or the colour of the sky. I decided to forget about it for a while.

▽ FINISHED PAINTING
Impression along the Grand Canal, Venice
Oil on canvas
76 × 101.6 cm (30 × 40 in)
Returning to the painting, I set about softening the buildings by using the broken brush technique and by modifying the colours. Only when the painting was finally balanced in terms of colour tones and brush work, was it finished.

effects, but in the process I wasn't happy with the larger buildings mass or the colour of the sky.

However, I framed the painting and hung it in the hall for two weeks, and forgot about it.

Making improvements

On return from holiday I looked at the painting again and decided immediately on what to do it improve it. I set about trying to soften the buildings mass in the left and right-hand sides of the composition by using the broken brush technique and by merging the brush strokes. This approach had the effect of giving the whole painting a consistent feel. I also enhanced the bottom of the sky by adding more lemon yellow and titanium white, which gave extra power and vibrancy to the picture. This gave extra contrast to the buildings in the background. To the left of the painting, I added broken brush work to the blue-covered areas and raised the tones of the blue to make the painting more vibrant.

Finally, I merged the roof areas of the background buildings with the sky, and I modified their colour and raised the shadow areas on the buildings with purple to give a better overall tonal harmony to the painting. These purple areas were also merged slightly with the surrounding colour to add consistency to the overall painting.

With the painting finally balanced in terms of colour tones and brush work, I felt that the painting was finished.

Setting the scene

In the previous two paintings, I had seen the subject and composition I wanted to paint. With *At the Garden Table*, my approach was different, as I hired some models and set up some scenes in my back garden. I had an idea for the models to be

△ INITIAL STAGE
At the Garden Table
With this painting, I set up the scene. Although I was happy with the composition and I liked the loose handling of paint, I felt it was lacking in detail and variations of colour.

around a table with lots of flowers and colours. Once I had found a composition I was happy with I painted in the main areas of the painting which resulted in the original picture

Although I liked the loose handling of paint I wanted the eye of the viewer almost to have an information overload with detail and variations of colour. In the original painting I felt the grass in the bottom right of the painting was the wrong hue. Having modified this, I then had to tone down the shade in the area and to a degree blend in the brush work in order to obtain a natural-looking balance.

I had problems with the tones of the tablecloth. Although wary of using pure white (I tend to take the edge off the white with a little lemon yellow), I was dissatisfied with the colour of the shade that I had created. The purple tone I had used was quite striking, but it really did not work in the painting at all. To modify this I set about making a greyer shadow which toned down the brightness of the purple, but still gave the impression of shade. This was also necessary to achieve with both models' dresses, which had light and shade areas.

Details and still life

I also needed to add details to the foliage and flowers in the background of the painting. Originally, I had painted the top left in an almost total black colour (the black having been created using French ultramarine and raw umber). However, I felt this looked a bit like a black hole, so I decided on a few slightly lighter leaves which contributed interest and a dimension to the area. With the background flowers I was keen to add the light impact to them. This was achieved by painting each flower with three tones, the lightest tone nearest to the light source, a medium tone, and a darker tone furthest from the light source. This gives a three-dimensional effect to the background and really makes the painting's colours 'sing out'.

As I wanted the painting to sing out it was important to get all the areas of light and shade accurate. I spent considerable time perfecting the still-life objects on the table, making sure the yellow flowers were vibrant and that the wine bottle had the correct light effects on it.

Tonal harmony

I was keen to make sure that the tonal harmony was correct on the flesh areas of the models, and this took quite a lot of work to get absolutely right. If the skin were too dark it would look out of place, even in shade: too bright, and the skin tones would look bleached. I was also acutely aware that the model on the right needed work on her hair, which was in a pony tail, as in the earlier stage it didn't really look like hair at all. I also paid close attention to the light on the chair and the position of the chair. This also took a great deal of work to get right as originally the chair legs were not correctly positioned.

Finally, I spent considerable time perfecting the other model's face. This was quite a key feature of the painting as a blank or badly painted face could quite easily ruin it. Once this was completed I made a final check over the whole work from a distance to make sure that I was happy with the details I had added.

△ **FINISHED PAINTING**
At the Garden Table
Oil on canvas
45.5 × 61 cm (18 × 24 in)
I decided to modify the grass, the shadows, the tablecloth and the models' dresses. I added details to the foliage and flowers and spent time perfecting the still-life objects. Once all of my revisions were completed I made a final check over the whole work from a distance to make sure I was happy with the result.

20 Relationships and scale

PETER GRAHAM

Two very different compositions presented the artist with various challenges, as is evident in this outdoor scene and still life.

Any painter will admit that every painting is a battleground. You may find yourself in the perfect spot on the perfect day, then halfway through the problem hits: perhaps the scale has been misjudged or the composition seems to focus too near to the edge so that the feet of the figures all disappear below the bottom of the page. And so it goes on. They say practice makes perfect, but in the case of painting the more you learn, the more you need to know. It seems an ever-expanding occupation. A couple of paintings completed recently in my studio can act as examples to show where, in my opinion, problems have occurred and how I have tackled them. These are trade secrets!

Looking at scale

Café du Jardin is a painting of a café terrace in a Paris garden. This is a studio painting worked up from various preliminary canvases painted on location. The early stages brought compositional challenges related to scale. One of my main focuses was the colour contrast of the parasols and lush greenery. The mood is carried with the bustle of the waiters and customers.

I love to have big areas of pure colour combined with perspective to lead the eye into the painting. The parasols started as slabs of cadmium yellow and the figures were added using swift strokes of greys and siennas.

Emphasizing the sun streaming in from the right as the painting progressed is the way I managed to define the depth. The use of a powerful yellow contrasting with terra rosa and powder blue accentuates the distances between tables and chairs. Capturing the glinting sun using lemon yellow and lime green on a bed of blue and sap green gives life to the sunlight dipping in and out of the chestnut canopy.

The use of lemon yellow mixed with a little titanium white created highlights for the figures seated at the tables, suggesting a dappling effect of sun filtering through the dense summer leaves.

Working with rapid strokes solved the dilemma of movement within the composition: even treating the trees and chairs with swift, vigorous brushwork helped to suggest the lively atmosphere, which was one of my main goals.

△ **STAGE ONE**
Establishing a suitable scale was the initial concern in this composition. I applied ground colours of Cadmium Yellow, Soft Grey and Blue to help suggest the afternoon heat.

The feeling of walking into a painting always appeals to me and in order to bring this off I developed the tone in the lower left-hand corner, using glazes of alizarin and magenta, suggesting shadow from a parasol, unseen, just outside the frame. This effect suggests an extra dimension beyond the canvas, so extending depth.

If there were no challenges in painting, it would not hold the fascination that it does. The ability to overcome difficulties in paint is the essence of the artist's work and solving problems leads to the development of a personal style and vision. There is always an answer to whatever you are attempting, so do not give up. A stubborn approach yields results, although it may create much frustration! Keeping an open mind and determined focus will bring solutions to problems and can transform a painting into a unique achievement.

△ DETAIL OF STAGE TWO
The waiter is a vitally important element in this composition. He draws the eye into the terrace of tables and by association invites us to sit at the table he is serving.

◁ FINISHED PAINTING
Café du Jardin
Oil on canvas
96.5 × 96.5 cm (38 × 38 in)
Using a series of Alizarin and Magenta glazes I developed the tone of the parasols and their shadows. This enhances the feeling of depth alongside detail picked out on the figures and adds to the dappled effect of sunlight falling on this bustle of activity.

Developing harmony

In the initial stages I like to shape out my
composition with broad brushstrokes using
thinned oils in order to cover the canvas without
paying too much attention to detail. In Stage one
of *Devon Lilies* (above), I laid down a warm ground
of sienna and ochre with strong gestural marks
anchoring the objects and picking out edges of
drapery that strengthen the composition. When
working with flowers I prefer, whenever possible, to
paint the objects first. This gives me the time I need
to develop depth of tone before bringing in the
fresh flowers, which may last only two or three days.

Strengthening relationships within the work
was the biggest problem I faced in this painting,
and a series of remedies helped to develop harmony
within the work. First, selecting a strong theme
between the objects, and using colour association,
allowed me to unify the surface of the painting.
Second, describing the interplay of sunlight
and shadow related the different objects to their
surroundings. Third, the use of overlap, particularly
with the flowers and drapery, has created the
illusion of depth – overlap is an important
technique that encourages the viewer to fill in the
missing parts of objects obscured behind others.
I find this leads to a more dynamic composition.

Colour, tone and mood

Playing with the hots and cools in a painting allows
the energy of colour to carry emotion. Here I have
used large swathes of cadmium yellow and scarlet,
producing a fierce heat right in the centre of the
composition. The soft blues of the Devonware
crockery bring both mood and tonal contrast. Bold
colour can also act as a magnificent shadow or echo
to the edge of a pot or jug, and push a shape forward.

Recognizing a successful effect in the
preliminary stages of a work and then enhancing it
can solve untold problems compositionally, so be
ready to preserve shapes or colours that appeal.
Early on in this painting I found that the strong red
silhouetting the teapot spout worked well, so it
stayed in place, even though it is a fairly raw mark.

I used a sable fan brush to merge the broken
colours together on the teapot, cups and jug. This

◁ **STAGE TWO**
Selecting a strong theme of blue Devonware crockery and relating that to background drapery unifies different parts of the painting through colour, and helps develop the mood of the work.

◁ **STAGE THREE**
Strengthening tone and enhancing reflection between objects takes the painting forward ready to bring in the lilies.

△ **FINISHED PAINTING**
Devon Lilies
Oil on canvas
66 × 68.5 cm (26 × 27 in)
Finally all the elements in
the work are brought into
focus using lively brushwork
to describe the flowers and
lead the eye around and into
the painting.

created a suitable ground to add just a few marks to
carry off the impression of a sphere. Once the main
objects in the still life had been defined it was time
to bring in the flowers.

The next challenge was how to tackle those
subtleties of line, colour, tone and mood that
flowers bring to a composition. Reflecting the
energy of the flowers was my aim, so I tried to keep
the marks fresh and lively with emphasis placed on
capturing the spontaneous effect of the light in the
lilies interacting with the cool blues of the setting,
and rendering the subtle variations that make up
each stem. The relationship between the flowers
and background can be helped by a well-placed
shadow which achieves both depth and association.

21 Too much colour?

TOM ROBB

To help you judge the most effective colour balance for a painting, the artist suggests experimenting with a restricted palette.

Sometimes you see an artist in a film or play who seems to achieve exactly the effect wanted in a picture with just a few flicks of the brush. Most of us know that this would be unusual, to put it mildly. Often we paint with false starts, crooked perspective and the composition out of kilter, and soon recognize that these are fundamental difficulties that, at worse, may not be correctable. A checklist of sorts can help; does the subject sit on the paper without looking cramped or too large? Are you pleased with the particular angle of the perspective? Does it look like an interesting idea? If all of these are positive, then chalk them up as a few large pluses: even if that individual painting has gone wrong you can think about rescuing an image which you know is exciting and worth the effort.

Taking a few hours away from the work while you do something else is always a good move, but if, even after this, you are still unhappy, then it is time to try to pinpoint what might be wrong with the first attempt.

All too often, the problem can be traced back to the colouring but not, perhaps, in the most obvious way. Even if you have been painting for only a short time, your eye will have learned whether a green, for example, is to yellow or too blue for what you want. It's relatively straightforward, once you start working with mixes and layering, to try out different combinations. But knowing how much colour to use is a more subtle skill, which can cause a great deal of anguish for new and experienced artists alike.

It is getting the balance right that can be tricky: not only the balance between the colours you are using, but also how much colour you need in the first place. Let's go back to the absolute minimum: black and white. Watercolour is not the best medium for this; the blacks are never quite black enough, even if the paper is a brilliant white. But the multifarious greys are another matter. Indeed, some of the most beautiful watercolours ever produced are almost completely grey.

Turner's later seascapes often look swathed in sea mist, or seen through evening clouds of stormy grey. Winslow Homer's misty paintings of a rower

△ **GREY VERSION**
Putney Bridge
Watercolour
40.5 × 49.5 cm (16 × 19 ½ in)
This scene has been painted over and over again, but each time it shows me something different. This version all in greys might well represent a quiet winter's day, the colour is leached out completely except for a few light touches of soft green on the leaves and a splatter of ochre here and there, and yet surely it is as convincing as any sketch done with every colour in the palette.

△ **RESTRAINED COLOUR**
Storm over the Deben
Watercolour
28 × 38 cm (11 × 15 in)
Here I worked with a little
more colour than in *Putney
Bridge* (page 119) but it was still
restrained; the thunderclouds
are hovering fairly low down
and the blue sky is still visible
in a few places. A touch, a very
light touch, of Indian red and
ochre brushes in the rain, with
ochre alone on the low-lying
fields and high on the clouds.
More colour would have
robbed the sketch completely
of its atmosphere.

on the river are nothing more than darker grey
shapes on a dark silver-steel surface. These artists
knew the subtle sheen of grey and its capacity to
transform an ordinary waterscape into a ghost of
its sunnier self. What could be a better place to start
seeing how much or how little a particular painting
might need?

A colour exercise

A useful exercise would be to devote a session to
painting a favourite landscape, using only greys.
This is more restricted than a monochrome in
sienna or blue; the effect will be quite different.
Then add just the least amount of colour you can
imagine to heighten the scene. Try this a few times
– it will give you a greater awareness of the power
of colour, and how it needs to be handled with
considerable respect.

Then move the target a little by adding more
touches of colour while still keeping the picture
based on grey. Stormy skies are a good choice and,
and also those wonderful hours between the dark

◁ **SKETCH**
Boats on the Beach
Watercolour and gouache
28 × 33 cm (11 × 13 in)
This is the sketch that started
the quest for a painting on a
brilliantly sunny day in
Portugal. It took only a few
minutes – the sun was so hot
the colour dried instantly, so
that the details of figures
and boats went on with a
little body colour.

and the daylight, which seems to suck almost all
the colour out of the light.

Having experimented with how little colour is
needed, it is time to handle bigger splashes and
brighter washes, while still keeping in mind that
less may be quite enough.

A day I spent painting on a beach in Portugal
(see *Boats on the Beach*, page 123) proved exactly how
important that basic premise is, yet how often it
gets ignored in the urge to capture a scene in all
its colourful glory. The morning produced a first
sketch (above) with some boats drawn up on the
sand while others were out to sea getting ready to
race; the result seemed just right, an incentive to
keep working.

Taking a stroll further down the beach, I could
envisage a larger painting as the next step; there
were brilliant sandstone cliffs which would add
drama and excitement. However in my first
attempt (*Boats on the Beach*: first mistake, page 122,
top) the heavy ultramarine (which was actually very
near the colour of the sky) completely overpowered

▷ STAGE ONE

The blue sky here seemed fine as it was washed on, but I soon realized that it was not right, even before adding the boat and the first shadowy figure. The cliffs looked about a mile away instead of rising up out of the beach just beyond the boat. Nothing was going to be able to compete with that blue.

▷ STAGE TWO

Correcting colours can go too far; the cliffs were right, but now the wishy-washy blue of the sky turned a sunny midday into a misty morning haze: luminous and with its own charm but so wrong for what was wanted. I decided to put it aside even before the hint of a figure or anything else was added.

the rest, so that the cliffs seemed to recede into the distance! I could have tried washing out the sky, but it was quicker and more satisfactory to begin again.

On a second attempt (above) the sky was much lighter but as soon as the cliffs were added, with all

their orange striations, the result was lovely and luminous but far from the hot, sun-drenched scene in front, and in my head. That sheet went to the back of the portfolio even more quickly! Turning away from the actual scene I did a colour trial with a quick splash of the paints. This helped to capture the two colours that did work together: just what was wanted.

Finally in the third attempt (above), the blue is strong enough to balance the cliffs, and the cliffs are sharp and clear enough to stand out as the impressive headland they are.

Respect for colour is vital – it needs to make its own statement, but it must also combine with and enhance other colours in the painting. Taking it away, element by element, will sometimes lead you to the perfect balance.

△ **FINISHED PAINTING**
Boats on the Beach:
Noon in Portugal
Watercolour and gouache
38 × 48 cm (15 × 19 in)
This is the final study, with the sky and the cliffs in harmony, each adding to the picture of a brilliantly hot summer's day. The minute the two main elements were on the paper it was clear this was a good colour balance, and the rest of the scene was finished quickly and easily. The next most important colour was the green foliage of the cliff face, and now this could be strong enough to sing out. A few dabs of body colour added highlights here and there over the paper. The darker sand in the foreground where the water slips away leaving damp patches, the walker cooling his feet in the shallow waves, the clusters of sunbathers and boatmen, are all part of the scene. Their vertical figures moving around keep the painting alive and vibrant – horizontal sunbathers would have made it feel far too sleepy!

Artists' biographies

Alastair C. Adams trained as an illustrator before developing an interest in figurative and portrait painting. He has gone on to exhibit and sell his work nationally and internationally. His dynamic but natural and unassuming portraits have gained him acclaim through many national exhibitions and societies. Alastair is also a member of the Royal Society of Portrait Painters, the Manchester Academy of Fine Art and the National Acrylic Painters Association.

Ray Balkwill studied at Exeter College of Art. He worked in advertising as an art director, but demand for his paintings led him to give up his job to become a professional artist. He has held numerous solo exhibitions and has shown in group exhibitions, including the Royal Institute of Painters in Watercolour, the Royal West of England Academy and the South West Academy of Fine and Applied Arts. Ray writes regularly for *The Artist* and his work features in many other magazines and books.

Paul Brown began exhibiting in London in 1992. Since then his work has developed significantly and he has built up a large and enthusiastic following. His landscape paintings are reminiscent of the impressionists. His Venetian canvases are generally more painterly, whereas, in contrast the more figurative painting uses a somewhat tighter handling. The painter is similar to Renoir in so far as he finds a continuity of style in conflict with different light effects, subjects and formats.

David Curtis ROI, RSMA was elected to the Royal College of Marine Arts in 1983 and became a member of the Royal Institute of Oil Painters in 1988. David is the author of *A Light Touch, the Landscape in Oils* and *The Landscape in Watercolour – A Personal View*. A regular exhibitor at the Richard Hagen Gallery in Broadway, Worcestershire, he also exhibits in all the major National Society exhibitions and has work held in private collections, both nationally and abroad.

Paul Derbyshire paints mainly in water-based media and regularly exhibits his work. He has won numerous prizes and Blackburn Museum & Art Gallery held an exhibition of his work in 2004. His work has featured in *The Artist* magazine and also *Modern & Contemporary Prints* by Phoebe Phillips and Tom Robb. Paul's paintings hang in private and corporate collections in the USA, UK and especially Hong Kong from where he finds most of his inspiration.

Peter Graham ROI studied at Glasgow School of Art. He has earned the reputation of being one of Britain's most gifted and distinctive Modern Colourists. His work is often related to the Modern Scottish School, but Peter has a flamboyant style which is unique – his detailed brush work combines with loose fluid strokes creating vibrant contrasts of pure colour, line and tone. A leading member of the Council of the Royal Institute of Oil Painters, Peter's work is held in public and private collections around the world and has received a number of major awards.

Gerald Green has worked as a professional artist since the mid-1980s, having previously practised as an architect. His reputation as one of Britain's leading architectural illustrators is well known and his clients have included large national and international property development companies. His watercolour and oil paintings are currently available at several galleries throughout England. Gerald is a regular contributor to *The Artist* magazine and his work has featured in five other books.

Hugo Grenville's studio paintings of the female figure reveal a striking spiritual intensity. In their exploration of line and colour, and celebration of pattern making, they peel back layers of feeling. His concern to communicate inner feeling also resonates in his landscapes. Hugo undertakes occasional portrait commissions, and lectures on painting at his Red House Studios summer school. He writes regularly on painting for *The Artist* magazine.

Barry Herniman MCSD had his first exhibition of watercolours in Ross-on-Wye in 1991 and took up painting full time in 1997. He has exhibited in England, Ireland, Canada and the USA, and was the winner of the SAA Artist of the Year Award 2001. Although favouring watercolour, Barry also enjoys working in pastels, acrylic and mixed media (pastel and watercolour). He is a regular feature writer for *The Artist* magazine and has produced two instructional videos.

Carol Hodgson gave up a place at art college in order to travel the world, but gained a comparable grounding through visiting different cultures and participating in various courses during her travels. She won a number of awards and prestigious commissions both in the USA and Hong Kong, and on her return to the UK worked for a time in the commercial sector. Carol now works nearly exclusively in pastel, preparing pieces for shows such as Patchings and The Great Sheffield Art Show. She organises an ever-expanding programme of workshops and demonstrations, and lives in Doncaster.

James Horton MA (RCA) RBA studied at the Royal College of Art Painting School (1971–74). He has had several solo exhibitions and his work has appeared in all the major National Society exhibitions up and down the country. James has written seven books including *Sketching with James Horton* and *Learn to Draw the Figure* for HarperCollins. He is a regular contributor to *The Artist* and has also contributed to *Art and Artists, Artist and Illustrator* and *Leisure Painter*.

John Lidzey was awarded the Daler-Rowney Prize at the Royal Watercolour Society Exhibition in 1990 and two years later he was a prize winner in the Singer Friedlander/*Sunday Times* Watercolour Competition. He regularly exhibits his work and many of his watercolours are in collections in the UK, the USA, Europe and Australia. A regular contributor to *The Artist*, he has produced two videos on watercolour painting, and written several popular books, including *Learn to Paint Light in Watercolour* and *Watercolour Workshop* for HarperCollins.

John Mitchell RSW, who trained at Edinburgh College of Art, is a member of the Royal Scottish Society of Painters in Watercolours and a professional member of the Society of Scottish Artists. He has shown watercolours and oils in one-man and group exhibitions throughout Scotland. Mountain landscapes and seascapes provide inspiration for many of his paintings. A regular contributor to *The Artist* magazine, he lives in Fife.

Anuk Naumann studied Architecture at University College, London, and qualified as an architect in 1975. While living and working in New York she studied silk-screen printing. Anuk paints a variety of subjects, with still life as her favourite. She works in water-based paints and increasingly uses collage in mixed media pieces. She has exhibited widely in England and Scotland and her paintings have been published as fine art prints.

Winston Oh learnt the watercolour technique from John Yardley RI and the late James Fletcher-Watson RI. He travels a great deal in the UK, Europe and the East in search of inspiration and variety of subjects. He is also enthusiastic about painting outdoors. He has written

instructional articles for *The Artist* magazine for many years, and teaches watercolours at Dedham Hall, Essex. He has exhibited in London, Colchester, Switzerland, and Singapore.

Darren Rees is a self-taught artist who mainly uses watercolour in the field, and acrylic and oil paint for larger landscapes and studio works. He has won many awards including BirdWatch Artist of the Year, Natural World Fine Art Award and the RSPB Fine Art Award. His book *Bird Impressions* was greeted by much critical acclaim. Darren is a member of the Society of Wildlife Artists and writes regularly for *Birds Illustrated* magazine.

Tom Robb NND, ARCA, MCSD, FSAE, FRSA studied at Carlisle College of Art and the Royal College of Art. He has been a practising teacher of art throughout his career and was Professor of Fine Art and Head of School at Middlesex University until his retirement. His work has been shown in solo and group exhibitions in various well-known galleries in London. Tom is the author of a number of practical art books and is a regular contributor to *The Artist* magazine and other publications.

Bob Rudd RI studied at the Bath Academy of Art (1969–73) and became a member of the Royal Society of Painters in Watercolours in 1995. He has exhibited extensively at galleries in London and throughout the country, including solo exhibitions in London, Edinburgh and the Isles of Scilly, collecting prestigious awards along the way. His work is displayed in public and corporate collections including the new parliamentary buildings at Westminster and the House of Lords.

Jackie Simmonds began to paint in her thirties, attending art school as a full-time mature student, and she is now a busy painter and art instruction author. Her work is exhibited regularly in both mixed exhibitions and one-woman shows, and reproductions of her work have been exhibited worldwide. Jackie writes regular articles for *The Artist* magazine, runs workshops and painting holidays, and has written five art instruction books and made six painting videos.

Olwen Tarrant was President of the Royal Institute of Oil Painters (ROI) (1999–2004). She won her first prize while still at the Sir John Cass College of Art in London – the first of many prizes and awards. Olwyn has appeared on radio and television, has written many articles for magazines and her paintings and drawings are featured in numerous art text books. She has lectured and demonstrated on painting in many parts of the country and regularly exhibits her work.

Further information

Some other addresses and websites you might find useful are:

Art magazines

The Artist
Caxton House
63/65 High Street
Tenterden
Kent TN30 6BD
www.theartistmagazine.co.uk

Leisure Painter
Caxton House
63/65 High Street
Tenterden
Kent TN30 6BD
www.leisurepainter.co.uk

Art materials

Daler-Rowney Limited
Bracknell
Berkshire RG12 8ST
Tel: 01344 424 621
www.daler-rowney.com

Winsor & Newton
Whitefriars Avenue
Wealdstone
Harrow
Middlesex HA3 5RH
Tel: 020 8427 4343
www.winsornewton.com

T.N. Lawrence & Son Limited
208 Portland Road
Hove BN3 5QT
Tel: 0845 644 3232
www.lawrence.co.uk

Jackson's Art Supplies
1 Farleigh Place
London N16 7SX
Tel: 020 7254 0077
www.jacksonsart.com

Bird & Davis Canvases
45 Holmes Road
London NW5 3AN
Tel: 020 7485 3797
www.birdanddavis.co.uk

Art societies

Royal Watercolour Society
Bankside Gallery
48 Hopton Street
London SE1 9JH
www.banksidegallery.com

Federation of British Artists
Mall Galleries
17 Carlton House Terrace
London SW1Y 5BD
Tel: 020 7930 6844
www.mallgalleries.org.uk

Bookclubs

Artists' Choice
P.O. Box 3
Huntingdon
Cambridgeshire PE28 0QX
Tel: 01832 710 201
www.artists-choice.co.uk

The Arts Guild Book Club
Greater London House
LondonNW1 7TZ
Tel: 020 7760 6500
www.artsguild.co.uk

Internet resources

Art Museum Network
The official website of the world's leading art museums.
www.amn.org

Artcourses
An easy way to find part-time classes, workshops and painting holidays. You can search by location, subject or duration.
www.artcourses.co.uk

British Arts
A useful resource with lots of information on all art-related matters.
www.britisharts.co.uk

Painters Online
An interactive art club for practising amateur and professional artists run by The Artist's Publishing Company.
www.painters-online.com

Videos

APV Films
6 Alexandra Square
Chipping Norton
Oxfordshire OX7 5HL
Tel: 01608 641 798
www.apvfilms.com

Teaching Art
P.O. Box 50
Newark
Nottinghamshire NG23 5GY
Tel: 01949 844 050
www.teachingart.com

Index

The next step

If you have enjoyed this book, why not have a look at other art instruction titles from Collins?

Collins Artist's Colour Manual
0-00-714703-1
hardback £20.00

Collins Art Class
0-00-712822-3
paperback £14.99

The Artist's Problem Solver
0-00-716571-4
paperback £12.99

The Artist's Watercolour Problem Solver
0-00-714948-4
hardback £16.99

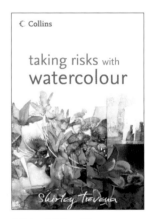

Taking Risks with Watercolour
0-00-713326-X
hardback £17.99

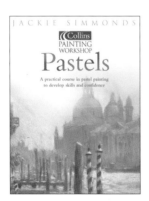

Painting Workshops Pastels
0-00-714257-9
paperback £12.99

Painting Workshops Watercolour
0-00-712167-9
paperback £12.99

Watercolour Innovations
0-00717782-8
hardback £17.99

To order any of these titles, please telephone 0870 787 1732.
For further information about Collins books, visit our website: www.collins.co.uk